THE RED ONE

Jack London

1st WORLD
LIBRARY
Literary Society

The Red One

Jack London

© 1st World Library, 2006
PO Box 2211
Fairfield, IA 52556
www.1stworldlibrary.com
First Edition

LCCN: 2006938074

Softcover ISBN: 978-1-4218-3373-6
Hardcover ISBN: 978-1-4218-3273-9
eBook ISBN: 978-1-4218-3473-3

Purchase *"The Red One"*
as a traditional bound book at:
www.1stWorldLibrary.com/purchase.asp?ISBN=978-1-4218-3373-6

1st World Library is a literary, educational organization
dedicated to:

- Creating a free internet library of downloadable ebooks

- Hosting writing competitions and offering book
  publishing scholarships.

Interested in more 1st World Library books?
contact: literacy@1stworldlibrary.com

Check us out at: www.1stworldlibrary.com

1ˢᵗ World Library Literary Society

Giving Back to the World

"If you want to work on the core problem, it's early school literacy."

- James Barksdale, former CEO of Netscape

"No skill is more crucial to the future of a child, or to a democratic and prosperous society, than literacy."

- Los Angeles Times

Literacy... means far more than learning how to read and write... The aim is to transmit... knowledge and promote social participation."

- UNESCO

"Literacy is not a luxury, it is a right and a responsibility. If our world is to meet the challenges of the twenty-first century we must harness the energy and creativity of all our citizens."

- President Bill Clinton

"Parents should be encouraged to read to their children, and teachers should be equipped with all available techniques for teaching literacy, so the varying needs and capacities of individual kids can be taken into account."

- Hugh Mackay

CONTENTS

THE RED ONE..7

THE HUSSY.. 35

LIKE ARGUS OF THE ANCIENT TIMES.............. 58

THE PRINCESS 90

THE RED ONE

There it was! The abrupt liberation of sound! As he timed it with his watch, Bassett likened it to the trump of an archangel. Walls of cities, he meditated, might well fall down before so vast and compelling a summons. For the thousandth time vainly he tried to analyse the tone-quality of that enormous peal that dominated the land far into the strong-holds of the surrounding tribes. The mountain gorge which was its source rang to the rising tide of it until it brimmed over and flooded earth and sky and air. With the wantonness of a sick man's fancy, he likened it to the mighty cry of some Titan of the Elder World vexed with misery or wrath. Higher and higher it arose, challenging and demanding in such profounds of volume that it seemed intended for ears beyond the narrow confines of the solar system. There was in it, too, the clamour of protest in that there were no ears to hear and comprehend its utterance.

- Such the sick man's fancy. Still he strove to analyse the sound. Sonorous as thunder was it, mellow as a golden bell, thin and sweet as a thrummed taut cord of silver—no; it was none of these, nor a blend of these. There were no words nor semblances in his vocabulary and experience with which to describe the totality of that sound.

Time passed. Minutes merged into quarters of hours, and quarters of hours into half-hours, and still the sound persisted, ever changing from its initial vocal impulse yet never receiving fresh impulse—fading, dimming, dying as enormously as it had sprung into being. It became a confusion of troubled mutterings and babblings and colossal whisperings. Slowly it withdrew, sob by sob, into whatever great bosom had birthed it, until it whimpered deadly whispers of wrath and as equally seductive whispers of delight, striving still to be heard, to convey some cosmic secret, some understanding of infinite import and value. It dwindled to a ghost of sound that had lost its menace and promise, and became a thing that pulsed on in the sick man's consciousness for minutes after it had ceased. When he could hear it no longer, Bassett glanced at his watch. An hour had elapsed ere that archangel's trump had subsided into tonal nothingness.

Was this, then, HIS dark tower?—Bassett pondered, remembering his Browning and gazing at his skeleton-like and fever-wasted hands. And the fancy made him smile—of Childe Roland bearing a slug-horn to his lips with an arm as feeble as his was. Was it months, or years, he asked himself, since he first heard that mysterious call on the beach at Ringmanu? To save himself he could not tell. The long sickness had been most long. In conscious count of time he knew of months, many of them; but he had no way of estimating the long intervals of delirium and stupor. And how fared Captain Bateman of the blackbirder Nari? he wondered; and had Captain Bateman's drunken mate died of delirium tremens yet?

From which vain speculations, Bassett turned idly to review all that had occurred since that day on the beach of Ringmanu when he first heard the sound and plunged into the jungle after it. Sagawa had protested. He could see him yet, his queer little monkeyish face eloquent with fear, his back burdened with specimen cases, in his hands Bassett's butterfly net and naturalist's shot-gun, as he quavered, in Beche-de-mer English: "Me fella too much fright along bush. Bad fella boy, too much stop'm along bush."

Bassett smiled sadly at the recollection. The little New Hanover boy had been frightened, but had proved faithful, following him without hesitancy into the bush in the quest after the source of the wonderful sound. No fire-hollowed tree-trunk, that, throbbing war through the jungle depths, had been Bassett's conclusion. Erroneous had been his next conclusion, namely, that the source or cause could not be more distant than an hour's walk, and that he would easily be back by mid-afternoon to be picked up by the Nari's whale-boat.

"That big fella noise no good, all the same devil-devil," Sagawa had adjudged. And Sagawa had been right. Had he not had his head hacked off within the day? Bassett shuddered. Without doubt Sagawa had been eaten as well by the "bad fella boys too much" that stopped along the bush. He could see him, as he had last seen him, stripped of the shot-gun and all the naturalist's gear of his master, lying on the narrow trail where he had been decapitated barely the moment before. Yes, within a minute the thing had happened. Within a minute, looking back, Bassett had seen him trudging patiently along under his burdens. Then Bassett's own trouble had come upon him. He looked at the cruelly healed stumps of the first and second fingers of his left hand, then rubbed them softly into the indentation in the back of his skull. Quick as had been the flash of the long handled tomahawk, he had been quick enough to duck away his head and partially to deflect the stroke with his up-flung hand. Two fingers and a hasty scalp-wound had been the price he paid for his life. With one barrel of his ten-gauge shot-gun he had blown the life out of the bushman who had so nearly got him; with the other barrel he had peppered the bushmen bending over Sagawa, and had the pleasure of knowing that the major portion of the charge had gone into the one who leaped away with Sagawa's head. Everything had occurred in a flash. Only himself, the slain bushman, and what remained of Sagawa, were in the narrow, wild-pig run of a path. From the dark jungle on either side came no rustle of movement or sound of life. And he had suffered distinct and dreadful shock. For the first time in his life he had killed a human being, and he knew nausea as he contemplated the mess of his handiwork.

Then had begun the chase. He retreated up the pig-run before his hunters, who were between him and the beach. How many there were, he could not guess. There might have been one, or a hundred, for aught he saw of them. That some of them took to the trees and travelled along through the jungle roof he was certain; but at the most he never glimpsed more than an occasional flitting of shadows. No bow-strings twanged that he could hear; but every little while, whence discharged he knew not, tiny arrows whispered past him or struck tree-boles and fluttered to the ground beside him. They were bone-tipped and feather shafted, and the feathers, torn from the breasts of humming-birds, iridesced like jewels.

Once—and now, after the long lapse of time, he chuckled gleefully at the recollection—he had detected a shadow above him that came to instant rest as he turned his gaze upward. He could make out nothing, but, deciding to chance it, had fired at it a heavy charge of number five shot. Squalling like an infuriated cat, the shadow crashed down through tree-ferns and orchids and thudded upon the earth at his feet, and, still squalling its rage and pain, had sunk its human teeth into the ankle of his stout tramping boot. He, on the other hand, was not idle, and with his free foot had done what reduced the squalling to silence. So inured to savagery has Bassett since become, that he chuckled again with the glee of the recollection.

What a night had followed! Small wonder that he had accumulated such a virulence and variety of fevers, he thought, as he recalled that sleepless night of torment, when the throb of his wounds was as nothing compared with the myriad stings of the mosquitoes. There had been no escaping them, and he had not dared to light a fire. They had literally pumped his body full of poison, so that, with the coming of day, eyes swollen almost shut, he had stumbled blindly on, not caring much when his head should be hacked off and his carcass started on the way of Sagawa's to the cooking fire. Twenty-four hours had made a wreck of him—of mind as well as body. He had scarcely retained his wits at all, so maddened was he by the tremendous inoculation of poison he had received. Several

Jack London

times he fired his shot-gun with effect into the shadows that dogged him. Stinging day insects and gnats added to his torment, while his bloody wounds attracted hosts of loathsome flies that clung sluggishly to his flesh and had to be brushed off and crushed off.

Once, in that day, he heard again the wonderful sound, seemingly more distant, but rising imperiously above the nearer war-drums in the bush. Right there was where he had made his mistake. Thinking that he had passed beyond it and that, therefore, it was between him and the beach of Ringmanu, he had worked back toward it when in reality he was penetrating deeper and deeper into the mysterious heart of the unexplored island. That night, crawling in among the twisted roots of a banyan tree, he had slept from exhaustion while the mosquitoes had had their will of him.

Followed days and nights that were vague as nightmares in his memory. One clear vision he remembered was of suddenly finding himself in the midst of a bush village and watching the old men and children fleeing into the jungle. All had fled but one. From close at hand and above him, a whimpering as of some animal in pain and terror had startled him. And looking up he had seen her—a girl, or young woman rather, suspended by one arm in the cooking sun. Perhaps for days she had so hung. Her swollen, protruding tongue spoke as much. Still alive, she gazed at him with eyes of terror. Past help, he decided, as he noted the swellings of her legs which advertised that the joints had been crushed and the great bones broken. He resolved to shoot her, and there the vision terminated. He could not remember whether he had or not, any more than could he remember how he chanced to be in that village, or how he succeeded in getting away from it.

Many pictures, unrelated, came and went in Bassett's mind as he reviewed that period of his terrible wanderings. He remembered invading another village of a dozen houses and driving all before him with his shot-gun save, for one old man, too feeble to flee, who spat at him and whined and snarled as he dug open a ground-oven and from amid the hot stones dragged forth a roasted pig that steamed its essence deliciously through its green-leaf wrappings. It was at this place that a wantonness of savagery had seized upon him. Having feasted, ready to depart with a hind-quarter of the pig in his hand, he deliberately fired the grass thatch of a house with his burning glass.

But seared deepest of all in Bassett's brain, was the dank and noisome jungle. It actually stank with evil, and it was always twilight. Rarely did a shaft of sunlight penetrate its matted roof a hundred feet overhead. And beneath that roof was an aerial ooze of vegetation, a monstrous, parasitic dripping of decadent life-forms that rooted in death and lived on death. And through all this he drifted, ever pursued by the flitting shadows of the anthropophagi, themselves ghosts of evil that dared not face him in battle but that knew that, soon or late, they would feed on him. Bassett remembered that at the time, in lucid moments, he had likened himself to a wounded bull pursued by plains' coyotes too cowardly to battle with him for the meat of him, yet certain of the inevitable end of him when they would be full gorged. As the bull's horns and stamping hoofs kept off the coyotes, so his shot-gun kept off these Solomon Islanders, these twilight shades of bushmen of the island of Guadalcanal.

Came the day of the grass lands. Abruptly, as if cloven by the sword of God in the hand of God, the jungle terminated. The edge of it, perpendicular and as black as the infamy of it, was a hundred feet up and down. And, beginning at the edge of it, grew the grass—sweet, soft, tender, pasture grass that would have delighted the eyes and beasts of any husbandman and that extended, on and on, for leagues and leagues of velvet verdure, to the backbone of the great island, the towering mountain range flung up by some ancient earth-cataclysm, serrated and gullied but not yet erased by the erosive tropic rains. But the grass! He had crawled into it a dozen yards, buried his face in it, smelled it, and broken down in a fit of involuntary weeping.

And, while he wept, the wonderful sound had pealed forth—if by PEAL, he had often thought since, an adequate description could be given of the enunciation of so vast a sound melting sweet. Sweet it was, as no sound ever heard. Vast it was, of so mighty a resonance that it might have proceeded from some brazen-throated monster. And yet it called to him across that leagues-wide savannah, and was like a benediction to his long-suffering, pain racked spirit.

He remembered how he lay there in the grass, wet-cheeked but no longer sobbing, listening to the sound and wondering that he had been able to hear it on the beach of Ringmanu. Some freak of air pressures and air currents, he reflected, had made it possible for the sound to carry so far. Such conditions might not happen again in a thousand days or ten thousand days, but the one day it had happened had been the day he landed from the Nari for several hours' collecting. Especially had he been in quest of the famed jungle butterfly, a foot across from wing-tip to wing-tip, as velvet-dusky of lack of colour as was the gloom of the roof, of such lofty arboreal habits that it resorted only to the jungle roof and could be brought down only by a dose of shot. It was for this purpose that Sagawa had carried the ten-gauge shot-gun.

Two days and nights he had spent crawling across that belt of grass land. He had suffered much, but pursuit had ceased at the jungle-edge. And he would have died of thirst had not a heavy thunderstorm revived him on the second day.

And then had come Balatta. In the first shade, where the savannah yielded to the dense mountain jungle, he had collapsed to die. At first she had squealed with delight at sight of his helplessness, and was for beating his brain out with a stout forest branch. Perhaps it was his very utter helplessness that had appealed to her, and perhaps it was her human curiosity that made her refrain. At any rate, she had refrained, for he opened his eyes again under the impending blow, and saw her studying him intently. What especially struck her about him were his blue eyes and white skin. Coolly she had squatted on her hams, spat on his arm, and with her finger-tips scrubbed away the dirt of days and nights of muck and jungle that sullied the pristine whiteness of his skin.

And everything about her had struck him especially, although there was nothing conventional about her at all. He laughed weakly at the recollection, for she had been as innocent of garb as Eve before the fig-leaf adventure. Squat and lean at the same time, asymmetrically limbed, string-muscled as if with lengths of cordage, dirt-caked from infancy save for casual showers, she was as unbeautiful a prototype of woman as he, with a scientist's eye, had ever gazed upon. Her breasts advertised at the one time her maturity and youth; and, if by nothing else, her sex was advertised by the one article of finery with which she was adorned, namely a pig's tail, thrust though a hole in her left ear-lobe. So lately had the tail been severed, that its raw end still oozed blood that dried upon her shoulder like so much candle-droppings. And her face! A twisted and wizened complex of apish features, perforated by upturned, sky-open, Mongolian nostrils, by a mouth that sagged from a huge upper-lip and faded precipitately into a retreating chin, by peering querulous eyes that blinked as blink the eyes of denizens of monkey-cages.

Not even the water she brought him in a forest-leaf, and the ancient and half-putrid chunk of roast pig, could redeem in the slightest the grotesque hideousness of her. When he had eaten weakly for a space, he closed his eyes in order not to see her, although again and again she poked them open to peer at the blue of them. Then had come the sound. Nearer, much nearer, he knew it to be; and he knew equally well, despite the weary way he had come, that it was still many hours distant. The effect of it on her had been startling. She cringed under it, with averted face, moaning and chattering with fear. But after it had lived its full life of an hour, he closed his eyes and fell asleep with Balatta brushing the flies from him.

When he awoke it was night, and she was gone. But he was aware of renewed strength, and, by then too thoroughly inoculated by the mosquito poison to suffer further inflammation, he closed his eyes and slept an unbroken stretch till sun-up. A little later Balatta had returned, bringing with her a half-dozen women who, unbeautiful as they were, were patently not so unbeautiful as she. She evidenced by her conduct that she considered him her find, her property, and the pride she took in showing him off would have been ludicrous had his situation not been so desperate.

Later, after what had been to him a terrible journey of miles, when he collapsed in front of the devil-devil house in the shadow of the breadfruit tree, she had shown very lively ideas on the matter of retaining possession of him. Ngurn, whom Bassett was to know afterward as the devil-devil doctor, priest, or medicine man of the village, had wanted his head. Others of the grinning and chattering monkey-men, all as stark of clothes and bestial of appearance as Balatta, had wanted his body for the roasting oven. At that time he had not understood their language, if by LANGUAGE might be dignified the uncouth sounds they made to represent ideas. But Bassett had thoroughly understood the matter of debate, especially when the men pressed and prodded and felt of the flesh of him as if he were so much commodity in a butcher's stall.

Balatta had been losing the debate rapidly, when the accident happened. One of the men, curiously examining Bassett's shotgun, managed to cock and pull a trigger. The recoil of the butt into the pit of the man's stomach had not been the most sanguinary result, for the charge of shot, at a distance of a yard, had blown the head of one of the debaters into nothingness.

Even Balatta joined the others in flight, and, ere they returned, his senses already reeling from the oncoming fever-attack, Bassett had regained possession of the gun. Whereupon, although his teeth chattered with the ague and his swimming eyes could scarcely see, he held on to his fading consciousness until he could intimidate the bushmen with the simple magics of compass, watch, burning glass, and matches. At the last, with due emphasis, of solemnity and awfulness, he had killed a young pig with his shot-gun and promptly fainted.

Bassett flexed his arm-muscles in quest of what possible strength might reside in such weakness, and dragged himself slowly and totteringly to his feet. He was shockingly emaciated; yet, during the various convalescences of the many months of his long sickness, he had never regained quite the same degree of strength as this time. What he feared was another relapse such as he had already frequently experienced. Without drugs, without even quinine, he had managed so far to live through a combination of the most pernicious and most malignant of malarial and black-water fevers. But could he continue to endure? Such was his everlasting query. For, like the genuine scientist he was, he would not be content to die until he had solved the secret of the sound.

Supported by a staff, he staggered the few steps to the devil-devil house where death and Ngurn reigned in gloom. Almost as infamously dark and evil-stinking as the jungle was the devil-devil house—in Bassett's opinion. Yet therein was usually to be found his favourite crony and gossip, Ngurn, always willing for a yarn or a discussion, the while he sat in the ashes of death and in a slow smoke shrewdly revolved curing human heads suspended from the rafters. For, through the months' interval of consciousness of his long sickness, Bassett had mastered the psychological simplicities and lingual difficulties of the language of the tribe of Ngurn and Balatta and Vngngn—the latter the addle-headed young chief who was ruled by Ngurn, and who, whispered intrigue had it, was the son of Ngurn.

"Will the Red One speak to-day?" Bassett asked, by this time so accustomed to the old man's gruesome occupation as to take even an interest in the progress of the smoke-curing.

With the eye of an expert Ngurn examined the particular head he was at work upon.

"It will be ten days before I can say 'finish,'" he said. "Never has any man fixed heads like these."

Bassett smiled inwardly at the old fellow's reluctance to talk with him of the Red One. It had always been so. Never, by any chance, had Ngurn or any other member of the weird tribe divulged the slightest hint of any physical characteristic of the Red One. Physical the Red One must be, to emit the wonderful sound, and though it was called the Red One, Bassett could not be sure that red represented the colour of it. Red enough were the deeds and powers of it, from what abstract clues he had gleaned. Not alone, had Ngurn informed him, was the Red One more bestial powerful than the neighbour tribal gods, ever athirst for the red blood of living human sacrifices, but the neighbour gods themselves were sacrificed and tormented before him. He was the god of a dozen allied villages similar to this one, which was the central and commanding village of the federation. By virtue of the Red One many alien villages had been devastated and even wiped out, the prisoners sacrificed to the Red One. This was true to-day, and it extended back into old history carried down by word of mouth through the generations. When he, Ngurn, had been a young man, the tribes beyond the grass lands had made a war raid. In the counter raid, Ngurn and his fighting folk had made many prisoners. Of children alone over five score living had been bled white before the Red One, and many, many more men and women.

The Thunderer was another of Ngurn's names for the mysterious deity. Also at times was he called The Loud Shouter, The God-Voiced, The Bird-Throated, The One with the Throat Sweet as the Throat of the Honey-Bird, The Sun Singer, and The Star-Born.

Why The Star-Born? In vain Bassett interrogated Ngurn. According to that old devil-devil doctor, the Red One had always been, just where he was at present, for ever singing and thundering his will over men. But Ngurn's father, wrapped in decaying grass-matting and hanging even then over their heads among the smoky rafters of the devil-devil house, had held otherwise. That departed wise one had believed that the Red One came from out of the starry night, else why—so his argument had run—had the old and forgotten ones passed his name down as the Star-Born? Bassett could not but recognize something cogent in such argument. But Ngurn affirmed the long years of his long life, wherein he had gazed upon many starry nights, yet never had he found a star on grass land or in jungle depth—and he had looked for them. True, he had beheld shooting stars (this in reply to Bassett's contention); but likewise had he beheld the phosphorescence of fungoid growths and rotten meat and fireflies on dark nights, and the flames of wood-fires and of blazing candle-nuts; yet what were flame and blaze and glow when they had flamed and blazed and glowed? Answer: memories, memories only, of things which had ceased to be, like memories of matings accomplished, of feasts forgotten, of desires that were the ghosts of desires, flaring, flaming, burning, yet unrealized in achievement of easement and satisfaction. Where was the appetite of yesterday? the roasted flesh of the wild pig the hunter's arrow failed to slay? the maid, unwed and dead ere the young man knew her?

A memory was not a star, was Ngurn's contention. How could a memory be a star? Further, after all his long life he still observed the starry night-sky unaltered. Never had he noted the absence of a single star from its accustomed place. Besides, stars were fire, and the Red One was not fire—which last involuntary betrayal told Bassett nothing.

"Will the Red One speak to-morrow?" he queried.

Ngurn shrugged his shoulders as who should say.

"And the day after?—and the day after that?" Bassett persisted.

"I would like to have the curing of your head," Ngurn changed the subject. "It is different from any other head. No devil-devil has a head like it. Besides, I would cure it well. I would take months and months. The moons would come and the moons would go, and the smoke would be very slow, and I should myself gather the materials for the curing smoke. The skin would not wrinkle. It would be as smooth as your skin now."

He stood up, and from the dim rafters, grimed with the smoking of countless heads, where day was no more than a gloom, took down a matting-wrapped parcel and began to open it.

"It is a head like yours," he said, "but it is poorly cured."

Bassett had pricked up his ears at the suggestion that it was a white man's head; for he had long since come to accept that these jungle-dwellers, in the midmost centre of the great island, had never had intercourse with white men. Certainly he had found them without the almost universal beche-de-mer English of the west South Pacific. Nor had they knowledge of tobacco, nor of gunpowder. Their few precious knives, made from lengths of hoop-iron, and their few and more precious tomahawks from cheap trade hatchets, he had surmised they had captured in war from the bushmen of the jungle beyond the grass lands, and that they, in turn, had similarly gained them from the salt-water men who fringed the coral beaches of the shore and had contact with the occasional white men.

"The folk in the out beyond do not know how to cure heads," old Ngurn explained, as he drew forth from the filthy matting and placed in Bassett's hands an indubitable white man's head.

Ancient it was beyond question; white it was as the blond hair attested. He could have sworn it once belonged to an English-man, and to an Englishman of long before by token of the heavy gold circlets still threaded in the withered ear-lobes.

"Now your head . . . " the devil-devil doctor began on his favourite topic.

"I'll tell you what," Bassett interrupted, struck by a new idea.

"When I die I'll let you have my head to cure, if, first, you take me to look upon the Red One."

"I will have your head anyway when you are dead," Ngurn rejected the proposition. He added, with the brutal frankness of the savage: "Besides, you have not long to live. You are almost a dead man now. You will grow less strong. In not many months I shall have you here turning and turning in the smoke. It is pleasant, through the long afternoons, to turn the head of one you have known as well as I know you. And I shall talk to you and tell you the many secrets you want to know. Which will not matter, for you will be dead."

"Ngurn," Bassett threatened in sudden anger. "You know the Baby Thunder in the Iron that is mine." (This was in reference to his all-potent and all-awful shotgun.) "I can kill you any time, and then you will not get my head."

"Just the same, will Vngngn, or some one else of my folk get it," Ngurn complacently assured him. "And just the same will it turn here in the and turn devil-devil house in the smoke. The quicker you slay me with your Baby Thunder, the quicker will your head turn in the smoke."

And Bassett knew he was beaten in the discussion.

What was the Red One?—Bassett asked himself a thousand times in the succeeding week, while he seemed to grow stronger. What was the source of the wonderful sound? What was this Sun Singer, this Star-Born One, this mysterious deity, as bestial-conducted as the black and kinky-headed and monkey-like human beasts who worshipped it, and whose silver-sweet, bull-mouthed singing and commanding he had heard at the taboo distance for so long?

Ngurn had he failed to bribe with the inevitable curing of his head when he was dead. Vngngn, imbecile and chief that he was, was too imbecilic, too much under the sway of Ngurn, to be considered. Remained Balatta, who, from the time she found him and poked his blue eyes open to recrudescence of her grotesque female hideousness, had continued his adorer. Woman she was, and he had long known that the only way to win from her treason of her tribe was through the woman's heart of her.

Bassett was a fastidious man. He had never recovered from the initial horror caused by Balatta's female awfulness. Back in England, even at best the charm of woman, to him, had never been robust. Yet now, resolutely, as only a man can do who is capable of martyring himself for the cause of science, he proceeded to violate all the fineness and delicacy of his nature by making love to the unthinkably disgusting bushwoman.

He shuddered, but with averted face hid his grimaces and swallowed his gorge as he put his arm around her dirt-crusted shoulders and felt the contact of her rancidoily and kinky hair with his neck and chin. But he nearly screamed when she succumbed to that caress so at the very first of the courtship and mowed and gibbered and squealed little, queer, pig-like gurgly noises of delight. It was too much. And the next he did in the singular courtship was to take her down to the stream and give her a vigorous scrubbing.

From then on he devoted himself to her like a true swain as frequently and for as long at a time as his will could override his repugnance. But marriage, which she ardently suggested, with due observance of tribal custom, he balked at. Fortunately, taboo rule was strong in the tribe. Thus, Ngurn could never touch bone, or flesh, or hide of crocodile. This had been ordained at his birth. Vngngn was denied ever the touch of woman. Such pollution, did it chance to occur, could be purged only by the death of the offending female. It had happened once, since Bassett's arrival, when a girl of nine, running in play, stumbled and fell against the sacred chief. And the girl-child was seen no more. In whispers, Balatta told Bassett that she had been three days and nights in dying before the Red One. As for Balatta, the breadfruit was taboo to her. For which Bassett was thankful. The taboo might have been water.

For himself, he fabricated a special taboo. Only could he marry, he explained, when the Southern Cross rode highest in the sky. Knowing his astronomy, he thus gained a reprieve of nearly nine months; and he was confident that within that time he would either be dead or escaped to the coast with full knowledge of the Red One and of the source of the Red One's wonderful voice. At first he had fancied the Red One to be some colossal statue, like Memnon, rendered vocal under certain temperature conditions of sunlight. But when, after a war raid, a batch of prisoners was brought in and the sacrifice made at night, in the midst of rain, when the sun could play no part, the Red One had been more vocal than usual, Bassett discarded that hypothesis.

In company with Balatta, sometimes with men and parties of women, the freedom of the jungle was his for three quadrants of the compass. But the fourth quadrant, which contained the Red One's abiding place, was taboo. He made more thorough love to Balatta—also saw to it that she scrubbed herself more frequently. Eternal female she was, capable of any treason for the sake of love. And, though the sight of her was provocative of nausea and the contact of her provocative of despair, although he could not escape her awfulness in his dream-haunted nightmares of her, he nevertheless was aware of the cosmic verity of sex that animated her and that made her own life of less value than the happiness of her lover with whom she hoped to mate. Juliet or Balatta? Where was the intrinsic difference? The soft and tender product of ultra-civilization, or her bestial prototype of a hundred thousand years before her?—there was no difference.

Bassett was a scientist first, a humanist afterward. In the jungle-heart of Guadalcanal he put the affair to the test, as in the laboratory he would have put to the test any chemical reaction. He increased his feigned ardour for the bushwoman, at the same time increasing the imperiousness of his will of desire over her to be led to look upon the Red One face to face. It was the old story, he recognized, that the woman must pay, and it occurred when the two of them, one day, were catching the unclassified and unnamed little black fish, an inch long, half-eel and half-scaled, rotund with salmon-golden roe, that frequented the fresh water, and that were esteemed, raw and whole, fresh or putrid, a perfect delicacy. Prone in the muck of the decaying jungle-floor, Balatta threw herself, clutching his ankles with her hands kissing his feet and making slubbery noises that chilled his backbone up and down again. She begged him to kill her rather than exact this ultimate love-payment. She told him of the penalty of breaking the taboo of the Red One—a week of torture, living, the details of which she yammered out from her face in the mire until he realized that he was yet a tyro in knowledge of the frightfulness the human was capable of wreaking on the human.

Yet did Bassett insist on having his man's will satisfied, at the woman's risk, that he might solve the mystery of the Red One's singing, though she should die long and horribly and screaming. And Balatta, being mere woman, yielded. She led him into the forbidden quadrant. An abrupt mountain, shouldering in from the north to meet a similar intrusion from the south, tormented the stream in which they had fished into a deep and gloomy gorge. After a mile along the gorge, the way plunged sharply upward until they crossed a saddle of raw limestone which attracted his geologist's eye. Still climbing, although he paused often from sheer physical weakness, they scaled forest-clad heights until they emerged on a naked mesa or tableland. Bassett recognized the stuff of its composition as black volcanic sand, and knew that a pocket magnet could have captured a full load of the sharply angular grains he trod upon.

And then holding Balatta by the hand and leading her onward, he came to it—a tremendous pit, obviously artificial, in the heart of the plateau. Old history, the South Seas Sailing Directions, scores of remembered data and connotations swift and furious, surged through his brain. It was Mendana who had discovered the islands and named them Solomon's, believing that he had found that monarch's fabled mines. They had laughed at the old navigator's child-like credulity; and yet here stood himself, Bassett, on the rim of an excavation for all the world like the diamond pits of South Africa.

But no diamond this that he gazed down upon. Rather was it a pearl, with the depth of iridescence of a pearl; but of a size all pearls of earth and time, welded into one, could not have totalled; and of a colour undreamed of in any pearl, or of anything else, for that matter, for it was the colour of the Red One. And the Red One himself Bassett knew it to be on the instant. A perfect sphere, full two hundred feet in diameter, the top of it was a hundred feet below the level of the rim. He likened the colour quality of it to lacquer. Indeed, he took it to be some sort of lacquer, applied by man, but a lacquer too marvellously clever to have been manufactured by the bush-folk. Brighter than bright cherry-red, its richness of colour was as if it were red builded upon red. It glowed and iridesced in the sunlight as if gleaming up from underlay under underlay of red.

In vain Balatta strove to dissuade him from descending. She threw herself in the dirt; but, when he continued down the trail that spiralled the pit-wall, she followed, cringing and whimpering her terror. That the red sphere had been dug out as a precious thing, was patent. Considering the paucity of members of the federated twelve villages and their primitive tools and methods, Bassett knew that the toil of a myriad generations could scarcely have made that enormous excavation.

He found the pit bottom carpeted with human bones, among which, battered and defaced, lay village gods of wood and stone. Some, covered with obscene totemic figures and designs, were carved from solid tree trunks forty or fifty feet in length. He noted the absence of the shark and turtle gods, so common among the shore villages, and was amazed at the constant recurrence of the helmet motive. What did these jungle savages of the dark heart of Guadalcanal know of helmets? Had

Mendana's men-at-arms worn helmets and penetrated here centuries before? And if not, then whence had the bush-folk caught the motive?

Advancing over the litter of gods and bones, Balatta whimpering at his heels, Bassett entered the shadow of the Red One and passed on under its gigantic overhang until he touched it with his finger-tips. No lacquer that. Nor was the surface smooth as it should have been in the case of lacquer. On the contrary, it was corrugated and pitted, with here and there patches that showed signs of heat and fusing. Also, the substance of it was metal, though unlike any metal, or combination of metals, he had ever known. As for the colour itself, he decided it to be no application. It was the intrinsic colour of the metal itself.

He moved his finger-tips, which up to that had merely rested, along the surface, and felt the whole gigantic sphere quicken and live and respond. It was incredible! So light a touch on so vast a mass! Yet did it quiver under the finger-tip caress in rhythmic vibrations that became whisperings and rustlings and mutterings of sound—but of sound so different; so elusively thin that it was shimmeringly sibilant; so mellow that it was maddening sweet, piping like an elfin horn, which last was just what Bassett decided would be like a peal from some bell of the gods reaching earthward from across space.

He looked at Balatta with swift questioning; but the voice of the Red One he had evoked had flung her face downward and moaning among the bones. He returned to contemplation of the prodigy. Hollow it was, and of no metal known on earth, was his conclusion. It was right-named by the ones of old-time as the Star-Born. Only from the stars could it have come, and no thing of chance was it. It was a creation of artifice and mind. Such perfection of form, such hollowness that it certainly possessed, could not be the result of mere fortuitousness. A child of intelligences, remote and unguessable, working corporally in metals, it indubitably was. He stared at it in amaze, his brain a racing wild-fire of hypotheses to account for this far-journeyer who had adventured the night of space, threaded the stars, and now rose before him and above him, exhumed by patient anthropophagi, pitted and lacquered by its fiery bath in two atmospheres.

But was the colour a lacquer of heat upon some familiar metal? Or was it an intrinsic quality of the metal itself? He thrust in the blue-point of his pocket-knife to test the constitution of the stuff. Instantly the entire sphere burst into a mighty whispering, sharp with protest, almost twanging goldenly, if a whisper could possibly be considered to twang, rising higher, sinking deeper, the two extremes of the registry of sound threatening to complete the circle and coalesce into the bull-mouthed thundering he had so often heard beyond the taboo distance.

Forgetful of safety, of his own life itself, entranced by the wonder of the unthinkable and unguessable thing, he raised his knife to strike heavily from a long stroke, but was prevented by Balatta. She upreared on her own knees in an agony of terror, clasping his knees and supplicating him to desist. In the intensity of her desire to impress him, she put her forearm between her teeth and sank them to the bone.

He scarcely observed her act, although he yielded automatically to his gentler instincts and withheld the knife-hack. To him, human life had dwarfed to microscopic proportions before this colossal portent of higher life from within the distances of the sidereal universe. As had she been a dog, he kicked the ugly little bushwoman to her feet and compelled her to start with him on an encirclement of the base. Part way around, he encountered horrors. Even, among the others, did he recognize the sun-shrivelled remnant of the nine-years girl who had accidentally broken Chief Vngngn's personality taboo. And, among what was left of these that had passed, he encountered what was left of one who had not yet passed. Truly had the bush-folk named themselves into the name of the Red One, seeing in him their own image which they strove to placate and please with such red offerings.

Jack London

Farther around, always treading the bones and images of humans and gods that constituted the floor of this ancient charnel-house of sacrifice, he came upon the device by which the Red One was made to send his call singing thunderingly across the jungle-belts and grass-lands to the far beach of Ringmanu. Simple and primitive was it as was the Red One's consummate artifice. A great king-post, half a hundred feet in length, seasoned by centuries of superstitious care, carven into dynasties of gods, each superimposed, each helmeted, each seated in the open mouth of a crocodile, was slung by ropes, twisted of climbing vegetable parasites, from the apex of a tripod of three great forest trunks, themselves carved into grinning and grotesque adumbrations of man's modern concepts of art and god. From the striker king-post, were suspended ropes of climbers to which men could apply their strength and direction. Like a battering ram, this king-post could be driven end-onward against the mighty red-iridescent sphere.

Here was where Ngurn officiated and functioned religiously for himself and the twelve tribes under him. Bassett laughed aloud, almost with madness, at the thought of this wonderful messenger, winged with intelligence across space, to fall into a bushman stronghold and be worshipped by ape-like, man-eating and head- hunting savages. It was as if God's World had fallen into the muck mire of the abyss underlying the bottom of hell; as if Jehovah's Commandments had been presented on carved stone to the monkeys of the monkey cage at the Zoo; as if the Sermon on the Mount had been preached in a roaring bedlam of lunatics.

The slow weeks passed. The nights, by election, Bassett spent on the ashen floor of the devil-devil house, beneath the ever-swinging, slow-curing heads. His reason for this was that it was taboo to the lesser sex of woman, and therefore, a refuge for him from Balatta, who grew more persecutingly and perilously loverly as the Southern Cross rode higher in the sky and marked the imminence of her nuptials. His days Bassett spent in a hammock swung under the shade of the great breadfruit tree before the devil-devil house. There were breaks in this programme, when, in the comas of his devastating fever-attacks, he lay for days and nights in the house of heads. Ever he struggled to combat the fever, to live, to continue to live, to grow strong and stronger against the day when he would be strong enough to dare the grass-lands and the belted jungle beyond, and win to the beach, and to some labour-recruiting, black-birding ketch or schooner, and on to civilization and the men of civilization, to whom he could give news of the message from other worlds that lay, darkly worshipped by beastmen, in the black heart of Guadalcanal's midmost centre.

On the other nights, lying late under the breadfruit tree, Bassett spent long hours watching the slow setting of the western stars beyond the black wall of jungle where it had been thrust back by the clearing for the village. Possessed of more than a cursory knowledge of astronomy, he took a sick man's pleasure in speculating as to the dwellers on the unseen worlds of those incredibly remote suns, to haunt whose houses of light, life came forth, a shy visitant, from the rayless crypts of matter. He could no more apprehend limits to time than bounds to space. No subversive radium speculations had shaken his steady scientific faith in the conservation of energy and the indestructibility of matter. Always and forever must there have been stars. And surely, in that cosmic ferment, all must be comparatively alike, comparatively of the same substance, or substances, save for the freaks of the ferment. All must obey, or compose, the same laws that ran without infraction through the entire experience of man. Therefore, he argued and agreed, must worlds and life be appanages to all the suns as they were appanages to the particular of his own solar system.

Even as he lay here, under the breadfruit tree, an intelligence that stared across the starry gulfs, so must all the universe be exposed to the ceaseless scrutiny of innumerable eyes, like his, though grantedly different, with behind them, by the same token, intelligences that questioned and sought the meaning and the construction of the whole. So reasoning, he felt his soul go forth in kinship with that august company, that multitude whose gaze was forever upon the arras of infinity.

Who were they, what were they, those far distant and superior ones who had bridged the sky with their gigantic, red-iridescent, heaven-singing message? Surely, and long since, had they, too, trod the path on which man had so recently, by the calendar of the cosmos, set his feet. And to be able to send a message across the pit of space, surely they had reached those heights to which man, in tears and travail and bloody sweat, in darkness and confusion of many counsels, was so slowly struggling. And what were they on their heights? Had they won Brotherhood? Or had they learned that the law of love imposed the penalty of weakness and decay? Was strife, life? Was the rule of all the universe the pitiless rule of natural selection? And, and most immediately and poignantly, were their far conclusions, their long-won wisdoms, shut even then in the huge, metallic heart of the Red One, waiting for the first earth-man to read? Of one thing he was certain: No drop of red dew shaken from the lion-mane of some sun in torment, was the sounding sphere. It was of design, not chance, and it contained the speech and wisdom of the stars.

What engines and elements and mastered forces, what lore and mysteries and destiny-controls, might be there! Undoubtedly, since so much could be enclosed in so little a thing as the foundation stone of a public building, this enormous sphere should contain vast histories, profounds of research achieved beyond man's wildest guesses, laws and formulae that, easily mastered, would make man's life on earth, individual and collective, spring up from its present mire to inconceivable heights of purity and power. It was Time's greatest gift to blindfold, insatiable, and sky-aspiring man. And to him, Bassett, had been vouchsafed the lordly fortune to be the first to receive this message from man's interstellar kin!

No white man, much less no outland man of the other bush-tribes, had gazed upon the Red One and lived. Such the law expounded by Ngurn to Bassett. There was such a thing as blood brotherhood. Bassett, in return, had often argued in the past. But Ngurn had stated solemnly no. Even the blood brotherhood was outside the favour of the Red One. Only a man born within the tribe could look upon the Red One and live. But now, his guilty secret known only to Balatta, whose fear of immolation before the Red One fast-sealed her lips, the situation was different. What he had to do was to recover from the abominable fevers that weakened him, and gain to civilization. Then would he lead an expedition back, and, although the entire population of Guadalcanal he destroyed, extract from the heart of the Red One the message of the world from other worlds.

But Bassett's relapses grew more frequent, his brief convalescences less and less vigorous, his periods of coma longer, until he came to know, beyond the last promptings of the optimism inherent in so tremendous a constitution as his own, that he would never live to cross the grass lands, perforate the perilous coast jungle, and reach the sea. He faded as the Southern Cross rose higher in the sky, till even Balatta knew that he would be dead ere the nuptial date determined by his taboo. Ngurn made pilgrimage personally and gathered the smoke materials for the curing of Bassett's head, and to him made proud announcement and exhibition of the artistic perfectness of his intention when Bassett should be dead. As for himself, Bassett was not shocked. Too long and too deeply had life ebbed down in him to bite him with fear of its impending extinction. He continued to persist, alternating periods of unconsciousness with periods of semi-consciousness, dreamy and unreal, in which he idly wondered whether he had ever truly beheld the Red One or whether it was a nightmare fancy of delirium.

Came the day when all mists and cob-webs dissolved, when he found his brain clear as a bell, and took just appraisement of his body's weakness. Neither hand nor foot could he lift. So little control of his body did he have, that he was scarcely aware of possessing one. Lightly indeed his flesh sat upon his soul, and his soul, in its briefness of clarity, knew by its very clarity that the black of cessation was near. He knew the end was close; knew that in all truth he had with his eyes beheld the Red One, the messenger between the worlds; knew that he would never live to carry that message to the world—that message, for aught to the contrary, which might already have waited man's hearing in the heart of Guadalcanal for ten thousand years. And Bassett stirred with resolve, calling Ngurn to him, out under the shade of the breadfruit tree, and with the old devil-devil doctor discussing the terms and arrangements of his last life effort, his final adventure in the quick of the flesh.

"I know the law, O Ngurn," he concluded the matter. "Whoso is not of the folk may not look upon the Red One and live. I shall not live anyway. Your young men shall carry me before the face of the Red One, and I shall look upon him, and hear his voice, and thereupon die, under your hand, O Ngurn. Thus will the three things be satisfied: the law, my desire, and your quicker possession of my head for which all your preparations wait."

To which Ngurn consented, adding:

"It is better so. A sick man who cannot get well is foolish to live on for so little a while. Also is it better for the living that he should go. You have been much in the way of late. Not but what it was good for me to talk to such a wise one. But for moons of days we have held little talk. Instead, you have taken up room in the house of heads, making noises like a dying pig, or talking much and loudly in your own language which I do not understand. This has been a confusion to me, for I like to think on the great things of the light and dark as I turn the heads in the smoke. Your much noise has thus been a disturbance to the long-learning and hatching of the final wisdom that will be mine before I die. As for you, upon whom the dark has already brooded, it is well that you die now. And I promise you, in the long days to come when I turn your head in the smoke, no man of the tribe shall come in to disturb us. And I will tell you many secrets, for I am an old man and very wise, and I shall be adding wisdom to wisdom as I turn your head in the smoke."

So a litter was made, and, borne on the shoulders of half a dozenof the men, Bassett departed on the last little adventure that was to cap the total adventure, for him, of living. With a body of which he was scarcely aware, for even the pain had been exhausted out of it, and with a bright clear brain that accommodated him to a quiet ecstasy of sheer lucidness of thought, he lay back on the lurching litter and watched the fading of the passing world, beholding for the last time the breadfruit tree before the devil-devil house, the dim day beneath the matted jungle roof, the gloomy gorge between the shouldering mountains, the saddle of raw limestone, and the mesa of black volcanic sand.

Down the spiral path of the pit they bore him, encircling the sheening, glowing Red One that seemed ever imminent to iridesce from colour and light into sweet singing and thunder. And over bones and logs of immolated men and gods they bore him, past the horrors of other immolated ones that yet lived, to the three-king-post tripod and the huge king-post striker.

Here Bassett, helped by Ngurn and Balatta, weakly sat up, swaying weakly from the hips, and with clear, unfaltering, all-seeing eyes gazed upon the Red One.

"Once, O Ngurn," he said, not taking his eyes from the sheening, vibrating surface whereon and wherein all the shades of cherry-redplayed unceasingly, ever a-quiver to change into sound, to become silken rustlings, silvery whisperings, golden thrummings of cords, velvet pipings of elfland, mellow distances of thunderings.

"I wait," Ngurn prompted after a long pause, the long-handled tomahawk unassumingly ready in his hand.

"Once, O Ngurn," Bassett repeated, "let the Red One speak so that I may see it speak as well as hear it. Then strike, thus, when I raise my hand; for, when I raise my hand, I shall drop my head forward and make place for the stroke at the base of my neck. But, O Ngurn, I, who am about to pass out of the light of day for ever, would like to pass with the wonder-voice of the Red One singing greatly in my ears."

"And I promise you that never will a head be so well cured as yours," Ngurn assured him, at the same time signalling the tribesmen to man the propelling ropes suspended from the king-post striker. "Your head shall be my greatest piece of work in the curing of heads."

Bassett smiled quietly to the old one's conceit, as the great carved log, drawn back through two-score feet of space, was released. The next moment he was lost in ecstasy at the abrupt and thunderous liberation of sound. But such thunder! Mellow it was with preciousness of all sounding metals. Archangels spoke in it; it was magnificently beautiful before all other sounds; it was invested with the intelligence of supermen of planets of other suns; it was the voice of God, seducing and commanding to be heard. And—the everlasting miracle of that interstellar metal! Bassett, with his own eyes, saw colour and colours transform into sound till the whole visible surface of the vast sphere was a-crawl and titillant and vaporous with what he could not tell was colour or was sound. In that moment the interstices of matter were his, and the interfusings and intermating transfusings of matter and force.

Time passed. At the last Bassett was brought back from his ecstasy by an impatient movement of Ngurn. He had quite forgotten the old devil-devil one. A quick flash of fancy brought a husky chuckle into Bassett's throat. His shot-gun lay beside him in the litter. All he had to do, muzzle to head, was to press the trigger and blow his head into nothingness.

But why cheat him? was Bassett's next thought. Head-hunting, cannibal beast of a human that was as much ape as human, nevertheless Old Ngurn had, according to his lights, played squarer than square. Ngurn was in himself a forerunner of ethics and contract, of consideration, and gentleness in man. No, Bassett decided; it would be a ghastly pity and an act of dishonour to cheat the old fellow at the last. His head was Ngurn's, and Ngurn's head to cure it would be.

And Bassett, raising his hand in signal, bending forward his head as agreed so as to expose cleanly the articulation to his taut spinal cord, forgot Balatta, who was merely a woman, a woman merely and only and undesired. He knew, without seeing, when the razor-edged hatchet rose in the air behind him. And for that instant, ere the end, there fell upon Bassett the shadows of the Unknown, a sense of impending marvel of the rending of walls before the imaginable. Almost, when he knew the blow had started and just ere the edge of steel bit the flesh and nerves it seemed that he gazed upon the serene face of the Medusa, Truth—And, simultaneous with the bite of the steel on the onrush of the dark, in a flashing instant of fancy, he saw the vision of his head turning slowly, always turning, in the devil-devil house beside the breadfruit tree.

Waikiki, Honolulu, May 22, 1916.

THE HUSSY

There are some stories that have to be true—the sort that cannot be fabricated by a ready fiction-reckoner. And by the same token there are some men with stories to tell who cannot be doubted. Such a man was Julian Jones. Although I doubt if the average reader of this will believe the story Julian Jones told me. Nevertheless I believe it. So thoroughly am I convinced of its verity that I am willing, nay, eager, to invest capital in the enterprise and embark personally on the adventure to a far land.

It was in the Australian Building at the Panama Pacific Exposition that I met him. I was standing before an exhibit of facsimiles of the record nuggets which had been discovered in the goldfields of the Antipodes. Knobbed, misshapen and massive, it was as difficult to believe that they were not real gold as it was to believe the accompanying statistics of their weights and values.

"That's what those kangaroo-hunters call a nugget," boomed over my shoulder directly at the largest of the specimens.

I turned and looked up into the dim blue eyes of Julian Jones. I looked up, for he stood something like six feet four inches in height. His hair, a wispy, sandy yellow, seemed as dimmed and faded as his eyes. It may have been the sun which had washed out his colouring; at least his face bore the evidence of a prodigious and ardent sun-burn which had long since faded to yellow. As his eyes turned from the exhibit and focussed on mine I noted a queer look in them as of one who vainly tries to recall some fact of supreme importance.

"What's the matter with it as a nugget?" I demanded.

The remote, indwelling expression went out of his eyes as he boomed

"Why, its size."

"It does seem large," I admitted. "But there's no doubt it's authentic. The Australian Government would scarcely dare—"

"Large!" he interrupted, with a sniff and a sneer.

"Largest ever discovered—" I started on.

"Ever discovered!" His dim eyes smouldered hotly as he proceeded. "Do you think that every lump of gold ever discovered has got into the newspapers and encyclopedias?"

"Well," I replied judicially, "if there's one that hasn't, I don't see how we're to know about it. If a really big nugget, or nugget-finder, elects to blush unseen—"

"But it didn't," he broke in quickly. "I saw it with my own eyes, and, besides, I'm too tanned to blush anyway. I'm a railroad man and I've been in the tropics a lot. Why, I used to be the colour of mahogany—real old mahogany, and have been taken for a blue-eyed Spaniard more than once—"

It was my turn to interrupt, and I did.

"Was that nugget bigger than those in there, Mr.—er—?"

"Jones, Julian Jones is my name."

He dug into an inner pocket and produced an envelope addressed to such a person, care of General Delivery, San

Francisco; and I, in turn, presented him with my card.

"Pleased to know you, sir," he said, extending his hand, his voice booming as if accustomed to loud noises or wide spaces. "Of course I've heard of you, seen your picture in the papers, and all that, and, though I say it that shouldn't, I want to say that I didn't care a rap about those articles you wrote on Mexico. You're wrong, all wrong. You make the mistake of all Gringos in thinking a Mexican is a white man. He ain't. None of them ain't—Greasers, Spiggoties, Latin-Americans and all the rest of the cattle. Why, sir, they don't think like we think, or reason, or act. Even their multiplication table is different. You think seven times seven is forty-nine; but not them. They work it out different. And white isn't white to them, either. Let me give you an example. Buying coffee retail for house-keeping in one-pound or ten-pound lots—"

"How big was that nugget you referred to?" I queried firmly. "As big as the biggest of those?"

"Bigger," he said quietly. "Bigger than the whole blamed exhibit of them put together, and then some." He paused and regarded me with a steadfast gaze. "I don't see no reason why I shouldn't go into the matter with you. You've got a reputation a man ought to be able to trust, and I've read you've done some tall skylarking yourself in out-of-the-way places. I've been browsing around with an eye open for some one to go in with me on the proposition."

"You can trust me," I said.

And here I am, blazing out into print with the whole story just as he told it to me as we sat on a bench by the lagoon before the Palace of Fine Arts with the cries of the sea gulls in our ears. Well, he should have kept his appointment with me. But I anticipate.

As we started to leave the building and hunt for a seat, a small woman, possibly thirty years of age, with a washed-out complexion of the farmer's wife sort, darted up to him in a bird-like way, for all the world like the darting veering gulls over our heads and fastened herself to his arm with the accuracy and dispatch and inevitableness of a piece of machinery.

"There you go!" she shrilled. "A-trottin' right off and never givin' me a thought."

I was formally introduced to her. It was patent that she had never heard of me, and she surveyed me bleakly with shrewd black eyes, set close together and as beady and restless as a bird's.

"You ain't goin' to tell him about that hussy?" she complained.

"Well, now, Sarah, this is business, you see," he argued plaintively. "I've been lookin' for a likely man this long while, and now that he's shown up it seems to me I got a right to give him the hang of what happened."

The small woman made no reply, but set her thin lips in a needle-like line. She gazed straight before her at the Tower of Jewels with so austere an expression that no glint of refracted sunlight could soften it. We proceeded slowly to the lagoon, managed to obtain an unoccupied seat, and sat down with mutual sighs of relief as we released our weights from our tortured sightseeing feet.

"One does get so mortal weary," asserted the small woman, almost defiantly.

Two swans waddled up from the mirroring water and investigated us. When their suspicions of our niggardliness or lack of peanuts had been confirmed, Jones half-turned his back on his life-partner and gave me his story.

"Ever been in Ecuador? Then take my advice—and don't. Though I take that back, for you and me might be hitting it for there together if you can rustle up the faith in me and the backbone in yourself for the trip. Well, anyway, it ain't so many years ago that I came ambling in there on a rusty, foul-bottomed, tramp collier from Australia, forty-three days from land to land. Seven knots was her speed when everything favoured, and we'd had a two weeks' gale to the north'ard of New Zealand, and broke our engines down for two days off Pitcairn Island.

"I was no sailor on her. I'm a locomotive engineer. But I'd made friends with the skipper at Newcastle an' come along as his guest for as far as Guayaquil. You see, I'd heard wages was 'way up on the American railroad runnin' from that place over the Andes to Quito. Now Guayaquil—"

"Is a fever-hole," I interpolated.

Julian Jones nodded.

"Thomas Nast died there of it within a month after he landed.—He was our great American cartoonist," I added.

"Don't know him," Julian Jones said shortly. "But I do know he wasn't the first to pass out by a long shot. Why, look you the way I found it. The pilot grounds is sixty miles down the river. 'How's the fever?' said I to the pilot who came aboard in the early morning. 'See that Hamburg barque,' said he, pointing to a sizable ship at anchor. 'Captain and fourteen men dead of it already, and the cook and two men dying right now, and they're the last left of her.'

"And by jinks he told the truth. And right then they were dying forty a day in Guayaquil of Yellow Jack. But that was nothing, as I was to find out. Bubonic plague and small-pox were raging, while dysentery and pneumonia were reducing the population, and the railroad was raging worst of all. I mean that. For them that insisted in riding on it, it was more dangerous than all the other diseases put together.

"When we dropped anchor off Guayaquil half a dozen skippers

from other steamers came on board to warn our skipper not to let any of his crew or officers go ashore except the ones he wanted to lose. A launch came off for me from Duran, which is on the other side of the river and is the terminal of the railroad. And it brought off a man that soared up the gangway three jumps at a time he was that eager to get aboard. When he hit the deck he hadn't time to speak to any of us. He just leaned out over the rail and shook his fist at Duran and shouted: 'I beat you to it! I beat you to it!'

"'Who'd you beat to it, friend?' I asked. 'The railroad,' he said, as he unbuckled the straps and took off a big '44 Colt's automatic from where he wore it handy on his left side under his coat, 'I staved as long as I agreed—three months—and it didn't get me. I was a conductor.'"

"And that was the railroad I was to work for. All of which was nothing to what he told me in the next few minutes. The road ran from sea level at Duran up to twelve thousand feet on Chimborazo and down to ten thousand at Quito on the other side the range. And it was so dangerous that the trains didn't run nights. The through passengers had to get off and sleep in the towns at night while the train waited for daylight. And each train carried a guard of Ecuadoriano soldiers which was the most dangerous of all. They were supposed to protect the train crews, but whenever trouble started they unlimbered their rifles and joined the mob. You see, whenever a train wreck occurred, the first cry of the spiggoties was 'Kill the Gringos!' They always did that, and proceeded to kill the train crew and whatever chance Gringo passengers that'd escaped being killed in the accident. Which is their kind of arithmetic, which I told you a while back as being different from ours.

"Shucks! Before the day was out I was to find out for myself that that ex-conductor wasn't lying. It was over at Duran. I was to take my run on the first division out to Quito, for which place I was to start next morning—only one through train running every twenty-four hours. It was the afternoon of my first day, along about four o'clock, when the boilers of the

Jack London

Governor Hancock exploded and she sank in sixty feet of water alongside the dock. She was the big ferry boat that carried the railroad passengers across the river to Guayaquil. It was a bad accident, but it was the cause of worse that followed. By half-past four, big trainloads began to arrive. It was a feast day and they'd run an excursion up country but of Guayaquil, and this was the crowd coming back.

"And the crowd—there was five thousand of them—wanted to get ferried across, and the ferry was at the bottom of the river, which wasn't our fault. But by the Spiggoty arithmetic, it was. 'Kill the Gringos!' shouts one of them. And right there the beans were spilled. Most of us got away by the skin of our teeth. I raced on the heels of the Master Mechanic, carrying one of his babies for him, for the locomotives that was just pulling out. You see, way down there away from everywhere they just got to save their locomotives in times of trouble, because, without them, a railroad can't be run. Half a dozen American wives and as many children were crouching on the cab floors along with the rest of us when we pulled out; and the Ecuadoriano soldiers, who should have been protecting our lives and property, turned loose with their rifles and must have given us all of a thousand rounds before we got out of range.

"We camped up country and didn't come back to clean up until next day. It was some cleaning. Every flat-car, box-car, coach, asthmatic switch engine, and even hand-car that mob of Spiggoties had shoved off the dock into sixty feet of water on top of the Governor Hancock. They'd burnt the round house, set fire to the coal bunkers, and made a scandal of the repair shops. Oh, yes, and there were three of our fellows they'd got that we had to bury mighty quick. It's hot weather all the time down there."

Julian Jones came to a full pause and over his shoulder studied the straight-before-her gaze and forbidding expression of his wife's face.

"I ain't forgotten the nugget," he assured me.

"Nor the hussy," the little woman snapped, apparently at the mud-hens paddling on the surface of the lagoon.

"I've been travelling toward the nugget right along—"

"There was never no reason for you to stay in that dangerous country," his wife snapped in on him.

"Now, Sarah," he appealed. "I was working for you right along." And to me he explained: "The risk was big, but so was the pay. Some months I earned as high as five hundred gold. And here was Sarah waiting for me back in Nebraska—"

"An' us engaged two years," she complained to the Tower of Jewels.

"—What of the strike, and me being blacklisted, and getting typhoid down in Australia, and everything," he went on. "And luck was with me on that railroad. Why, I saw fellows fresh from the States pass out, some of them not a week on their first run. If the diseases and the railroad didn't get them, then it was the Spiggoties got them. But it just wasn't my fate, even that time I rode my engine down to the bottom of a forty-foot washout. I lost my fireman; and the conductor and the Superintendent of Rolling Stock (who happened to be running down to Duran to meet his bride) had their heads knifed off by the Spiggoties and paraded around on poles. But I lay snug as a bug under a couple of feet of tender coal, and they thought I'd headed for tall timber—lay there a day and a night till the excitement cooled down. Yes, I was lucky. The worst that happened to me was I caught a cold once, and another time had a carbuncle. But the other fellows! They died like flies, what of Yellow Jack, pneumonia, the Spiggoties, and the railroad. The trouble was I didn't have much chance to pal with them. No sooner'd I get some intimate with one of them he'd up and die—all but a fireman named Andrews, and he went loco for keeps.

"I made good on my job from the first, and lived in Quito in a 'dobe house with whacking big Spanish tiles on the roof that I'd rented. And I never had much trouble with the Spiggoties, what of letting them sneak free rides in the tender or on the cowcatcher. Me throw them off? Never! I took notice, when Jack Harris put off a bunch of them, that I attended his funeral muy pronto—"

"Speak English," the little woman beside him snapped.

"Sarah just can't bear to tolerate me speaking Spanish," he apologized. "It gets so on her nerves that I promised not to. Well, as I was saying, the goose hung high and everything was going hunky-dory, and I was piling up my wages to come north to Nebraska and marry Sarah, when I run on to Vahna—"

"The hussy!" Sarah hissed.

"Now, Sarah," her towering giant of a husband begged, "I just got to mention her or I can't tell about the nugget.—It was one night when I was taking a locomotive—no train—down to Amato, about thirty miles from Quito. Seth Manners was my fireman. I was breaking him in to engineer for himself, and I was letting him run the locomotive while I sat up in his seat meditating about Sarah here. I'd just got a letter from her, begging as usual for me to come home and hinting as usual about the dangers of an unmarried man like me running around loose in a country full of senoritas and fandangos. Lord! If she could only a-seen them. Positive frights, that's what they are, their faces painted white as corpses and their lips red as—as some of the train wrecks I've helped clean up.

"It was a lovely April night, not a breath of wind, and a tremendous big moon shining right over the top of Chimborazo.— Some mountain that. The railroad skirted it twelve thousand feet above sea level, and the top of it ten thousand feet higher than that.

"Mebbe I was drowsing, with Seth running the engine; but he

slammed on the brakes so sudden hard that I darn near went through the cab window.

"'What the—' I started to yell, and 'Holy hell,' Seth says, as both of us looked at what was on the track. And I agreed with Seth entirely in his remark. It was an Indian girl—and take it from me, Indians ain't Spiggoties by any manner of means. Seth had managed to fetch a stop within twenty feet of her, and us bowling down hill at that! But the girl. She—"

I saw the form of Mrs. Julian Jones stiffen, although she kept her gaze fixed balefully upon two mud-hens that were prowling along the lagoon shallows below us. "The hussy!" she hissed, once and implacably. Jones had stopped at the sound, but went on immediately.

"She was a tall girl, slim and slender, you know the kind, with black hair, remarkably long hanging, down loose behind her, as she stood there no more afraid than nothing, her arms spread out to stop the engine. She was wearing a slimpsy sort of garment wrapped around her that wasn't cloth but ocelot skins, soft and dappled, and silky. It was all she had on—"

"The hussy!" breathed Mrs. Jones.

But Mr. Jones went on, making believe that he was unaware of the interruption.

"Hell of a way to stop a locomotive," I complained at Seth, as I climbed down on to the right of way. I walked past our engine and up to the girl, and what do you think? Her eyes were shut tight. She was trembling that violent that you would see it by the moonlight. And she was barefoot, too.

"'What's the row?' I said, none too gentle. She gave a start, seemed to come out of her trance, and opened her eyes. Say! They were big and black and beautiful. Believe me, she was some looker—"

"The hussy!" At which hiss the two mud-hens veered away a few feet. But Jones was getting himself in hand, and didn't even blink.

"'What are you stopping this locomotive for?' I demanded in Spanish. Nary an answer. She stared at me, then at the snorting engine and then burst into tears, which you'll admit is uncommon behaviour for an Indian woman.

"'If you try to get rides that way,' I slung at her in Spiggoty Spanish (which they tell me is some different from regular Spanish), 'you'll be taking one smeared all over our cowcatcher and headlight, and it'll be up to my fireman to scrape you off.'"

"My Spiggoty Spanish wasn't much to brag on, but I could see she understood, though she only shook her head and wouldn't speak. But great Moses, she was some looker—"

I glanced apprehensively at Mrs. Jones, who must have caught me out of the tail of her eye, for she muttered: "If she hadn't been do you think he'd a-taken her into his house to live?"

"Now hold on, Sarah," he protested. "That ain't fair. Besides, I'm telling this.—Next thing, Seth yells at me, 'Goin' to stay here all night?'

"'Come on,' I said to the girl, 'and climb on board. But next time you want a ride don't flag a locomotive between stations.' She followed along; but when I got to the step and turned to give her a lift-up, she wasn't there. I went forward again. Not a sign of her. Above and below was sheer cliff, and the track stretched ahead a hundred yards clear and empty. And then I spotted her, crouched down right against the cowcatcher, that close I'd almost stepped on her. If we'd started up, we'd have run over her in a second. It was all so nonsensical, I never could make out her actions. Maybe she was trying to suicide. I grabbed her by the wrist and jerked her none too gentle to her feet. And she came along all right. Women do know when a man means business."

I glanced from this Goliath to his little, bird-eyed spouse, and wondered if he had ever tried to mean business with her.

"Seth kicked at first, but I boosted her into the cab and made her sit up beside me—"

"And I suppose Seth was busy running the engine," Mrs. Jones observed.

"I was breaking him in, wasn't I?" Mr. Jones protested. "So we made the run into Amato. She'd never opened her mouth once, and no sooner'd the engine stopped than she'd jumped to the ground and was gone. Just like that. Not a thank you kindly. Nothing.

"But next morning when we came to pull out for Quito with a dozen flat cars loaded with rails, there she was in the cab waiting for us; and in the daylight I could see how much better a looker she was than the night before.

"'Huh! she's adopted you,' Seth grins. And it looked like it. She just stood there and looked at me—at us—like a loving hound dog that you love, that you've caught with a string of sausages inside of him, and that just knows you ain't going to lift a hand to him. 'Go chase yourself!' I told her pronto." (Mrs. Jones her proximity noticeable with a wince at the Spanish word.) "You see, Sarah, I'd no use for her, even at the start."

Mrs. Jones stiffened. Her lips moved soundlessly, but I knew to what syllables.

"And what made it hardest was Seth jeering at me. 'You can't shake her that way,' he said. 'You saved her life—' 'I didn't,' I said sharply; 'it was you.' 'But she thinks you did, which is the same thing,' he came back at me. 'And now she belongs to you. Custom of the country, as you ought to know.'"

"Heathenish," said Mrs. Jones, and though her steady gaze was set upon the Tower of Jewels I knew she was making no reference to its architecture.

"'She's come to do light housekeeping for you,' Seth grinned. I let him rave, though afterwards I kept him throwing in the coal too fast to work his mouth very much. Why, say, when I got to the spot where I picked her up, and stopped the train for her to get off, she just flopped down on her knees, got a hammerlock with her arms around my knees, and cried all over my shoes. What was I to do?"

With no perceptible movement that I was aware of, Mrs. Jones advertised her certitude of knowledge of what SHE would have done.

"And the moment we pulled into Quito, she did what she'd done before—vanished. Sarah never believes me when I say how relieved I felt to be quit of her. But it was not to be. I got to my 'dobe house and managed a cracking fine dinner my cook had ready for me. She was mostly Spiggoty and half Indian, and her name was Paloma.—Now, Sarah, haven't I told you she was older'n a grandmother, and looked more like a buzzard than a dove? Why, I couldn't bear to eat with her around where I could look at her. But she did make things comfortable, and she was some economical when it came to marketing.

"That afternoon, after a big long siesta, what'd I find in the kitchen, just as much at home as if she belonged there, but that blamed Indian girl. And old Paloma was squatting at the girl's feet and rubbing the girl's knees and legs like for rheumatism, which I knew the girl didn't have from the way I'd sized up the walk of her, and keeping time to the rubbing with a funny sort of gibberish chant. And I let loose right there and then. As Sarah knows, I never could a-bear women around the house—young, unmarried women, I mean. But it was no go! Old Paloma sided with the girl, and said if the girl went she went, too. Also, she called me more kinds of a fool than the English language has accommodation for. You'd like the

Spanish lingo, Sarah, for expressing yourself in such ways, and you'd have liked old Paloma, too. She was a good woman, though she didn't have any teeth and her face could kill a strong man's appetite in the cradle.

"I gave in. I had to. Except for the excuse that she needed Vahna's help around the house (which she didn't at all), old Paloma never said why she stuck up for the girl. Anyway, Vahna was a quiet thing, never in the way. And she never gadded. Just sat in-doors jabbering with Paloma and helping with the chores. But I wasn't long in getting on to that she was afraid of something. She would look up, that anxious it hurt, whenever anybody called, like some of the boys to have a gas or a game of pedro. I tried to worm it out of Paloma what was worrying the girl, but all the old woman did was to look solemn and shake her head like all the devils in hell was liable to precipitate a visit on us.

"And then one day Vahna had a visitor. I'd just come in from a run and was passing the time of day with her—I had to be polite, even if she had butted in on me and come to live in my house for keeps—when I saw a queer expression come into her eyes. In the doorway stood an Indian boy. He looked like her, but was younger and slimmer. She took him into the kitchen and they must have had a great palaver, for he didn't leave until after dark. Inside the week he came back, but I missed him. When I got home, Paloma put a fat nugget of gold into my hand, which Vahna had sent him for. The blamed thing weighed all of two pounds and was worth more than five hundred dollars. She explained that Vahna wanted me to take it to pay for her keep. And I had to take it to keep peace in the house.

"Then, after a long time, came another visitor. We were sitting before the fire—"

"Him and the hussy," quoth Mrs. Jones.

"And Paloma," he added quickly.

"Him and his cook and his light housekeeper sitting by the fire," she amended.

"Oh, I admit Vahna did like me a whole heap," he asserted recklessly, then modified with a pang of caution: "A heap more than was good for her, seeing that I had no inclination her way.

"Well, as I was saying, she had another visitor. He was a lean, tall, white-headed old Indian, with a beak on him like an eagle. He walked right in without knocking. Vahna gave a little cry that was half like a yelp and half like a gasp, and flumped down on her knees before me, pleading to me with deer's eyes and to him with the eyes of a deer about to be killed that don't want to be killed. Then, for a minute that seemed as long as a life-time, she and the old fellow glared at each other. Paloma was the first to talk, in his own lingo, for he talked back to her. But great Moses, if he wasn't the high and mighty one! Paloma's old knees were shaking, and she cringed to him like a hound dog. And all this in my own house! I'd have thrown him out on his neck, only he was so old.

"If the things he said to Vahna were as terrible as the way he looked! Say! He just spit words at her! But Paloma kept whimpering and butting in, till something she said got across, because his face relaxed. He condescended to give me the once over and fired some question at Vahna. She hung her head, and looked foolish, and blushed, and then replied with a single word and a shake of the head. And with that he just naturally turned on his heel and beat it. I guess she'd said 'No.'

"For some time after that Vahna used to fluster up whenever she saw me. Then she took to the kitchen for a spell. But after a long time she began hanging around the big room again. She was still mighty shy, but she'd keep on following me about with those big eyes of hers—"

"The hussy!" I heard plainly. But Julian Jones and I were pretty well used to it by this time.

"I don't mind saying that I was getting some interested myself —oh, not in the way Sarah never lets up letting me know she thinks. That two-pound nugget was what had me going. If Vahna'd put me wise to where it came from, I could say good-bye to railroading and hit the high places for Nebraska and Sarah.

"And then the beans were spilled . . . by accident. Come a letter from Wisconsin. My Aunt Eliza 'd died and up and left me her big farm. I let out a whoop when I read it; but I could have canned my joy, for I was jobbed out of it by the courts and lawyers afterward—not a cent to me, and I'm still paying 'm in instalments.

"But I didn't know, then; and I prepared to pull back to God's country. Paloma got sore, and Vahna got the weeps. 'Don't go! Don't go!' That was her song. But I gave notice on my job, and wrote a letter to Sarah here—didn't I, Sarah?

"That night, sitting by the fire like at a funeral, Vahna really loosened up for the first time.

"'Don't go,' she says to me, with old Paloma nodding agreement with her. 'I'll show you where my brother got the nugget, if you don't go.' 'Too late,' said I. And I told her why.

"And told her about me waiting for you back in Nebraska," Mrs. Jones observed in cold, passionless tones.

"Now, Sarah, why should I hurt a poor Indian girl's feelings? Of course I didn't.

"Well, she and Paloma talked Indian some more, and then Vahna says: 'If you stay, I'll show you the biggest nugget that is the father of all other nuggets.' 'How big?' I asked. 'As big as me?' She laughed. 'Bigger than you,' she says, 'much, much bigger.' 'They don't grow that way,' I said. But she said she'd seen it and Paloma backed her up. Why, to listen to them you'd have thought there was millions in that one nugget.

Paloma 'd never seen it herself, but she'd heard about it. A secret of the tribe which she couldn't share, being only half Indian herself."

Julian Jones paused and heaved a sigh.

"And they kept on insisting until I fell for—"

"The hussy," said Mrs. Jones, pert as a bird, at the ready instant.

"No; for the nugget. What of Aunt Eliza's farm I was rich enough to quit railroading, but not rich enough to turn my back on big money—and I just couldn't help believing them two women. Gee! I could be another Vanderbilt, or J. P. Morgan. That's the way I thought; and I started in to pump Vahna. But she wouldn't give down. 'You come along with me,' she says. 'We can be back here in a couple of weeks with all the gold the both of us can carry.' 'We'll take a burro, or a pack-train of burros,' was my suggestion. But nothing doing. And Paloma agreed with her. It was too dangerous. The Indians would catch us."

"The two of us pulled out when the nights were moonlight. We travelled only at night, and laid up in the days. Vahna wouldn't let me light a fire, and I missed my coffee something fierce. We got up in the real high mountains of the main Andes, where the snow on one pass gave us some trouble; but the girl knew the trails, and, though we didn't waste any time, we were a full week getting there. I know the general trend of our travel, because I carried a pocket compass; and the general trend is all I need to get there again, because of that peak. There's no mistaking it. There ain't another peak like it in the world. Now, I'm not telling you its particular shape, but when you and I head out for it from Quito I'll take you straight to it.

"It's no easy thing to climb, and the person doesn't live that can climb it at night. We had to take the daylight to it, and didn't reach the top till after sunset. Why, I could take hours and hours telling you about that last climb, which I won't. The top was flat as a billiard table, about a quarter of an acre in size, and was almost clean of snow. Vahna told me that the great winds that usually blew, kept the snow off of it.

"We were winded, and I got mountain sickness so bad that I had to stretch out for a spell. Then, when the moon come up, I took a prowl around. It didn't take long, and I didn't catch a sight or a smell of anything that looked like gold. And when I asked Vahna, she only laughed and clapped her hands. Meantime my mountain sickness tuned up something fierce, and I sat down on a big rock to wait for it to ease down.

"'Come on, now,' I said, when I felt better. 'Stop your fooling and tell me where that nugget is.' 'It's nearer to you right now than I'll ever get,' she answered, her big eyes going sudden wistful. 'All you Gringos are alike. Gold is the love of your heart, and women don't count much.'"

"I didn't say anything. That was no time to tell her about Sarah here. But Vahna seemed to shake off her depressed feelings, and began to laugh and tease again. 'How do you like it?' she asked. 'Like what?' 'The nugget you're sitting on.'

"I jumped up as though it was a red-hot stove. And all it was was a rock. I felt nay heart sink. Either she had gone clean loco or this was her idea of a joke. Wrong on both counts. She gave me the hatchet and told me to take a hack at the boulder, which I did, again and again, for yellow spots sprang up from under every blow. By the great Moses! it was gold! The whole blamed boulder!"

Jones rose suddenly to his full height and flung out his long arms, his face turned to the southern skies. The movement shot panic into the heart of a swan that had drawn nearer with amiably predatory designs. Its consequent abrupt retreat collided it with a stout old lady, who squealed and dropped her bag of peanuts. Jones sat down and resumed.

"Gold, I tell you, solid gold and that pure and soft that I chopped chips out of it. It had been coated with some sort of rain-proof paint or lacquer made out of asphalt or something. No wonder I'd taken it for a rock. It was ten feet long, all of five feet through, and tapering to both ends like an egg. Here. Take a look at this."

From his pocket he drew and opened a leather case, from which he took an object wrapped in tissue-paper. Unwrapping it, he dropped into my hand a chip of pure soft gold, the size of a ten-dollar gold-piece. I could make out the greyish substance on one side with which it had been painted.

"I chopped that from one end of the thing," Jones went on, replacing the chip in its paper and leather case. "And lucky I put it in my pocket. For right at my back came one loud word—more like a croak than a word, in my way of thinking. And there was that lean old fellow with the eagle beak that had dropped in on us one night. And there was about thirty Indians with him—all slim young fellows.

"Vahna'd flopped down and begun whimpering, but I told her, 'Get up and make friends with them for me.' 'No, no,' she cried. 'This is death. Good-bye, amigo—'"

Here Mrs. Jones winced, and her husband abruptly checked the particular flow of his narrative.

"'Then get up and fight along with me,' I said to her. And she did. She was some hellion, there on the top of the world, clawing and scratching tooth and nail—a regular she cat. And I wasn't idle, though all I had was that hatchet and my long arms. But they were too many for me, and there was no place for me to put my back against a wall. When I come to, minutes after they'd cracked me on the head—here, feel this."

Removing his hat, Julian Jones guided my finger tips through his thatch of sandy hair until they sank into an indentation. It was fully three inches long, and went into the bone itself of the skull.

"When I come to, there was Vahna spread-eagled on top of the nugget, and the old fellow with a beak jabbering away solemnly as if going through some sort of religious exercises. In his hand he had a stone knife—you know, a thin, sharp sliver of some obsidian-like stuff same as they make arrow-heads out of. I couldn't lift a hand, being held down, and being too weak besides. And—well, anyway, that stone knife did for her, and me they didn't even do the honour of killing there on top their sacred peak. They chucked me off of it like so much carrion.

"And the buzzards didn't get me either. I can see the moonlight yet, shining on all those peaks of snow, as I went down. Why, sir, it was a five-hundred-foot fall, only I didn't make it. I went into a big snow-drift in a crevice. And when I come to (hours after I know, for it was full day when I next saw the sun), I found myself in a regular snow-cave or tunnel caused by the water from the melting snow running along the ledge. In fact, the stone above actually overhung just beyond where I first landed. A few feet more to the side, either way, and I'd almost be going yet. It was a straight miracle, that's what it was.

"But I paid for it. It was two years and over before I knew what happened. All I knew was that I was Julian Jones and that I'd been blacklisted in the big strike, and that I was married to Sarah here. I mean that. I didn't know anything in between, and when Sarah tried to talk about it, it gave me pains in the head. I mean my head was queer, and I knew it was queer.

"And then, sitting on the porch of her father's farmhouse back in Nebraska one moonlight evening, Sarah came out and put that gold chip into my hand. Seems she'd just found it in the torn lining of the trunk I'd brought back from Ecuador—I who for two years didn't even know I'd been to Ecuador, or Australia, or anything! Well, I just sat there looking at the chip in the moonlight, and turning it over and over and figuring what it was and where it'd come from, when all of a sudden there was a snap inside my head as if something had broken, and then I could see Vahna spread-eagled on that big nugget and the old fellow with the beak waving the stone knife, and . . . and everything. That is, everything that had happened from the time I first left Nebraska to when I crawled to the daylight out of the snow after they had chucked me off the mountain-top. But everything that'd happened after that I'd clean forgotten. When Sarah said I was her husband, I wouldn't listen to her. Took all her family and the preacher that'd married us to convince me.

"Later on I wrote to Seth Manners. The railroad hadn't killed him yet, and he pieced out a lot for me. I'll show you his letters. I've got them at the hotel. One day, he said, making his regular run, I crawled out on to the track. I didn't stand upright, I just crawled. He took me for a calf, or a big dog, at first. I wasn't anything human, he said, and I didn't know him or anything. As near as I can make out, it was ten days after the mountain-top to the time Seth picked me up. What I ate I don't know. Maybe I didn't eat. Then it was doctors at Quito, and Paloma nursing me (she must have packed that gold chip in my trunk), until they found out I was a man without a mind, and the railroad sent me back to Nebraska. At any rate, that's what Seth writes me. Of myself, I don't know. But Sarah here knows. She corresponded with the railroad before they shipped me and all that."

Mrs. Jones nodded affirmation of his words, sighed and evidenced unmistakable signs of eagerness to go.

"I ain't been able to work since," her husband continued. "And I ain't been able to figure out how to get back that big nugget. Sarah's got money of her own, and she won't let go a penny—"

"He won't get down to THAT country no more!" she broke forth.

"But, Sarah, Vahna's dead—you know that," Julian Jones protested.

"I don't know anything about anything," she answered decisively, "except that THAT country is no place for a married man."

Her lips snapped together, and she fixed an unseeing stare across to where the afternoon sun was beginning to glow into sunset. I gazed for a moment at her face, white, plump, tiny, and implacable, and gave her up.

"How do you account for such a mass of gold being there?" I queried of Julian Jones. "A solid-gold meteor that fell out of the sky?"

"Not for a moment." He shook his head. " It was carried there by the Indians."

"Up a mountain like that—and such enormous weight and size!" I objected.

"Just as easy," he smiled. "I used to be stumped by that proposition myself, after I got my memory back. Now how in Sam Hill—' I used to begin, and then spend hours figuring at it. And then when I got the answer I felt downright idiotic, it was that easy." He paused, then announced: "They didn't."

"But you just—said they did."

"They did and they didn't," was his enigmatic reply. "Of course they never carried that monster nugget up there. What they did was to carry up its contents."

He waited until he saw enlightenment dawn in my face.

"And then of course melted all the gold, or welded it, or smelted it, all into one piece. You know the first Spaniards down there, under a leader named Pizarro, were a gang of robbers and cut-throats. They went through the country like the hoof-and-mouth disease, and killed the Indians off like cattle. You see, the Indians had lots of gold. Well, what the Spaniards didn't get, the surviving Indians hid away in that one big chunk on top the mountain, and it's been waiting there ever since for me—and for you, if you want to go in on it."

And here, by the Lagoon of the Palace of Fine Arts, ended my acquaintance with Julian Jones. On my agreeing to finance the adventure, he promised to call on me at my hotel next morning with the letters of Seth Manners and the railroad, and conclude arrangements. But he did not call. That evening I telephoned his hotel and was informed by the clerk that Mr. Julian Jones and wife had departed in the early afternoon, with their baggage.

Can Mrs. Jones have rushed him back and hidden him away in Nebraska? I remember that as we said good-bye, there was that in her smile that recalled the vulpine complacency of Mona Lisa, the Wise.

Kohala, Hawaii, May 5, 1916.

LIKE ARGUS OF THE ANCIENT TIMES

It was the summer of 1897, and there was trouble in the Tarwater family. Grandfather Tarwater, after remaining properly subdued and crushed for a quiet decade, had broken out again. This time it was the Klondike fever. His first and one unvarying symptom of such attacks was song. One chant only he raised, though he remembered no more than the first stanza and but three lines of that. And the family knew his feet were itching and his brain was tingling with the old madness, when he lifted his hoarse-cracked voice, now falsetto-cracked, in:

> Like Argus of the ancient times,
> We leave this modern Greece,
> Tum-tum, tum-tum, tum, tum, tum-tum,
> To shear the Golden Fleece.

Ten years earlier he had lifted the chant, sung to the air of the "Doxology," when afflicted with the fever to go gold-mining in Patagonia. The multitudinous family had sat upon him, but had had a hard time doing it. When all else had failed to shake his resolution, they had applied lawyers to him, with the threat of getting out guardianship papers and of confining him in the state asylum for the insane—which was reasonable for a man who had, a quarter of a century before, speculated away all but ten meagre acres of a California principality, and who had displayed no better business acumen ever since.

The application of lawyers to John Tarwater was like the application of a mustard plaster. For, in his judgment, they were the gentry, more than any other, who had skinned him out of the broad Tarwater acres. So, at the time of his Patagonian fever, the very thought of so drastic a remedy was sufficient to cure him. He quickly demonstrated he was not crazy by shaking the fever from him and agreeing not to go to Patagonia.

Next, he demonstrated how crazy he really was, by deeding over to his family, unsolicited, the ten acres on Tarwater Flat, the house, barn, outbuildings, and water-rights. Also did he turn over the eight hundred dollars in bank that was the long-saved salvage of his wrecked fortune. But for this the family found no cause for committal to the asylum, since such committal would necessarily invalidate what he had done.

"Grandfather is sure peeved," said Mary, his oldest daughter, herself a grandmother, when her father quit smoking.

All he had retained for himself was a span of old horses, a mountain buckboard, and his one room in the crowded house. Further, having affirmed that he would be beholden to none of them, he got the contract to carry the United States mail, twice a week, from Kelterville up over Tarwater Mountain to Old Almaden—which was a sporadically worked quick-silver mine in the upland cattle country. With his old horses it took all his time to make the two weekly round trips. And for ten years, rain or shine, he had never missed a trip. Nor had he failed once to pay his week's board into Mary's hand. This board he had insisted on, in the convalescence from his Patagonian fever, and he had paid it strictly, though he had given up tobacco in order to be able to do it.

"Huh!" he confided to the ruined water wheel of the old Tarwater Mill, which he had built from the standing timber and which had ground wheat for the first settlers. "Huh! They'll never put me in the poor farm so long as I support myself. And without a penny to my name it ain't likely any lawyer fellows'll come snoopin' around after me."

And yet, precisely because of these highly rational acts, it was held that John Tarwater was mildly crazy!

The first time he had lifted the chant of "Like Argus of the Ancient Times," had been in 1849, when, twenty-two years' of age, violently attacked by the Californian fever, he had sold two hundred and forty Michigan acres, forty of it cleared, for the price of four yoke of oxen, and a wagon, and had started across the Plains.

"And we turned off at Fort Hall, where the Oregon emigration went north'ard, and swung south for Californy," was his way of concluding the narrative of that arduous journey. "And Bill Ping and me used to rope grizzlies out of the underbrush of Cache Slough in the Sacramento Valley."

Years of freighting and mining had followed, and, with a stake gleaned from the Merced placers, he satisfied the land-hunger of his race and time by settling in Sonoma County.

During the ten years of carrying the mail across Tarwater Township, up Tarwater Valley, and over Tarwater Mountain, most all of which land had once been his, he had spent his time dreaming of winning back that land before he died. And now, his huge gaunt form more erect than it had been for years, with a glinting of blue fires in his small and close-set eyes, he was lifting his ancient chant again.

"There he goes now—listen to him," said William Tarwater.

"Nobody at home," laughed Harris Topping, day labourer, husband of Annie Tarwater, and father of her nine children.

The kitchen door opened to admit the old man, returning from feeding his horses. The song had ceased from his lips; but Mary was irritable from a burnt hand and a grandchild whose stomach refused to digest properly diluted cows' milk.

"Now there ain't no use you carryin' on that way, father," she tackled him. "The time's past for you to cut and run for a place like the Klondike, and singing won't buy you nothing."

"Just the same," he answered quietly. "I bet I could go to that Klondike place and pick up enough gold to buy back the Tarwater lands."

"Old fool!" Annie contributed.

"You couldn't buy them back for less'n three hundred thousand and then some," was William's effort at squelching him.

"Then I could pick up three hundred thousand, and then some, if I was only there," the old man retorted placidly.

"Thank God you can't walk there, or you'd be startin', I know," Mary cried. "Ocean travel costs money."

"I used to have money," her father said humbly.

"Well, you ain't got any now—so forget it," William advised. "Them times is past, like roping bear with Bill Ping. There ain't no more bear."

"Just the same—"

But Mary cut him off. Seizing the day's paper from the kitchen table, she flourished it savagely under her aged progenitor's nose.

"What do those Klondikers say? There it is in cold print. Only the young and robust can stand the Klondike. It's worse than the north pole. And they've left their dead a-plenty there themselves. Look at their pictures. You're forty years older 'n the oldest of them."

John Tarwater did look, but his eyes strayed to other photographs on the highly sensational front page.

"And look at the photys of them nuggets they brought down," he said. "I know gold. Didn't I gopher twenty thousand outa the Merced? And wouldn't it a-ben a hundred thousand if that cloudburst hadn't busted my wing-dam? Now if I was only in the Klondike—"

"Crazy as a loon," William sneered in open aside to the rest.

"A nice way to talk to your father," Old Man Tarwater censured mildly. "My father'd have walloped the tar out of me with a single-tree if I'd spoke to him that way."

"But you ARE crazy, father—" William began.

"Reckon you're right, son. And that's where my father wasn't crazy. He'd a-done it."

"The old man's been reading some of them magazine articles about men who succeeded after forty," Annie jibed.

"And why not, daughter?" he asked. "And why can't a man succeed after he's seventy? I was only seventy this year. And mebbe I could succeed if only I could get to the Klondike—"

"Which you ain't going to get to," Mary shut him off.

"Oh, well, then," he sighed, "seein's I ain't, I might just as well go to bed."

He stood up, tall, gaunt, great-boned and gnarled, a splendid ruin of a man. His ragged hair and whiskers were not grey but snowy white, as were the tufts of hair that stood out on the backs of his huge bony fingers. He moved toward the door, opened it, sighed, and paused with a backward look.

"Just the same," he murmured plaintively, "the bottoms of my feet is itching something terrible."

Long before the family stirred next morning, his horses fed and harnessed by lantern light, breakfast cooked and eaten by lamp light, Old Man Tarwater was off and away down Tarwater Valley on the road to Kelterville. Two things were unusual about this usual trip which he had made a thousand and forty times since taking the mail contract. He did not drive to Kelterville, but turned off on the main road south to Santa Rosa. Even more remarkable than this was the paper-wrapped parcel between his feet. It contained his one decent black suit, which Mary had been long reluctant to see him wear any more, not because it was shabby, but because, as he guessed what was at the back of her mind, it was decent enough to bury him in.

And at Santa Rosa, in a second-hand clothes shop, he sold the suit outright for two dollars and a half. From the same obliging shopman he received four dollars for the wedding ring of his long-dead wife. The span of horses and the wagon he disposed of for seventy-five dollars, although twenty-five was all he received down in cash. Chancing to meet Alton Granger on the street, to whom never before had he mentioned the ten dollars loaned him in '74, he reminded Alton Granger of the little affair, and was promptly paid. Also, of all unbelievable men to be in funds, he so found the town drunkard for whom he had bought many a drink in the old and palmy days. And from him John Tarwater borrowed a dollar. Finally, he took the afternoon train to San Francisco.

A dozen days later, carrying a half-empty canvas sack of blankets and old clothes, he landed on the beach of Dyea in the thick of the great Klondike Rush. The beach was screaming bedlam. Ten thousand tons of outfit lay heaped and scattered, and twice ten thousand men struggled with it and clamoured about it. Freight, by Indian-back, over Chilcoot to Lake Linderman, had jumped from sixteen to thirty cents a pound, which latter was a rate of six hundred dollars a ton. And the sub-arctic winter gloomed near at hand. All knew it, and all knew that of the twenty thousand of them very few would get across the passes, leaving the rest to winter and wait for the late spring thaw.

Such the beach old John Tarwater stepped upon; and straight across the beach and up the trail toward Chilcoot he headed, cackling his ancient chant, a very Grandfather Argus himself, with no outfit worry in the world, for he did not possess any outfit. That night he slept on the flats, five miles above Dyea, at the head of canoe navigation. Here the Dyea River became a rushing mountain torrent, plunging out of a dark canyon from the glaciers that fed it far above.

And here, early next morning, he beheld a little man weighing no more than a hundred, staggering along a foot-log under all of a hundred pounds of flour strapped on his back. Also, he beheld the little man stumble off the log and fall face-downward in a quiet eddy where the water was two feet deep and proceed quietly to drown. It was no desire of his to take death so easily, but the flour on his back weighed as much as he and would not let him up.

"Thank you, old man," he said to Tarwater, when the latter had dragged him up into the air and ashore.

While he unlaced his shoes and ran the water out, they had further talk. Next, he fished out a ten-dollar gold-piece and offered it to his rescuer.

Old Tarwater shook his head and shivered, for the ice-water had wet him to his knees.

"But I reckon I wouldn't object to settin' down to a friendly meal with you."

"Ain't had breakfast?" the little man, who was past forty and who had said his name was Anson, queried with a glance frankly curious.

"Nary bite," John Tarwater answered.

"Where's your outfit? Ahead?"

Jack London

"Nary outfit."

"Expect to buy your grub on the Inside?"

"Nary a dollar to buy it with, friend. Which ain't so important as a warm bite of breakfast right now."

In Anson's camp, a quarter of a mile on, Tarwater found a slender, red-whiskered young man of thirty cursing over a fire of wet willow wood. Introduced as Charles, he transferred his scowl and wrath to Tarwater, who, genially oblivious, devoted himself to the fire, took advantage of the chill morning breeze to create a draught which the other had left stupidly blocked by stones, and soon developed less smoke and more flame. The third member of the party, Bill Wilson, or Big Bill as they called him, came in with a hundred-and-forty-pound pack; and what Tarwater esteemed to be a very rotten breakfast was dished out by Charles. The mush was half cooked and mostly burnt, the bacon was charred carbon, and the coffee was unspeakable.

Immediately the meal was wolfed down the three partners took their empty pack-straps and headed down trail to where the remainder of their outfit lay at the last camp a mile away. And old Tarwater became busy. He washed the dishes, foraged dry wood, mended a broken pack-strap, put an edge on the butcher-knife and camp-axe, and repacked the picks and shovels into a more carryable parcel.

What had impressed him during the brief breakfast was the sort of awe in which Anson and Big Bill stood of Charles. Once, during the morning, while Anson took a breathing spell after bringing in another hundred-pound pack, Tarwater delicately hinted his impression.

"You see, it's this way," Anson said. "We've divided our leadership. We've got specialities. Now I'm a carpenter. When we get to Lake Linderman, and the trees are chopped and whipsawed into planks, I'll boss the building of the boat. Big

Bill is a logger and miner. So he'll boss getting out the logs and all mining operations. Most of our outfit's ahead. We went broke paying the Indians to pack that much of it to the top of Chilcoot. Our last partner is up there with it, moving it along by himself down the other side. His name's Liverpool, and he's a sailor. So, when the boat's built, he's the boss of the outfit to navigate the lakes and rapids to Klondike.

"And Charles—this Mr. Crayton—what might his speciality be?" Tarwater asked.

"He's the business man. When it comes to business and organization he's boss."

"Hum," Tarwater pondered. "Very lucky to get such a bunch of specialities into one outfit."

"More than luck," Anson agreed. "It was all accident, too. Each of us started alone. We met on the steamer coming up from San Francisco, and formed the party.—Well, I got to be goin'. Charles is liable to get kicking because I ain't packin' my share' just the same, you can't expect a hundred-pound man to pack as much as a hundred-and-sixty-pounder."

"Stick around and cook us something for dinner," Charles, on his next load in and noting the effects of the old man's handiness, told Tarwater.

And Tarwater cooked a dinner that was a dinner, washed the dishes, had real pork and beans for supper, and bread baked in a frying-pan that was so delectable than the three partners nearly foundered themselves on it. Supper dishes washed, he cut shavings and kindling for a quick and certain breakfast fire, showed Anson a trick with foot-gear that was invaluable to any hiker, sang his "Like Argus of the Ancient Times," and told them of the great emigration across the Plains in Forty-nine.

"My goodness, the first cheerful and hearty-like camp since we hit the beach," Big Bill remarked as he knocked out his pipe and began pulling off his shoes for bed.

"Kind of made things easy, boys, eh?" Tarwater queried genially.

All nodded. "Well, then, I got a proposition, boys. You can take it or leave it, but just listen kindly to it. You're in a hurry to get in before the freeze-up. Half the time is wasted over the cooking by one of you that he might be puttin' in packin' outfit. If I do the cookin' for you, you all'll get on that much faster. Also, the cookin' 'll be better, and that'll make you pack better. And I can pack quite a bit myself in between times, quite a bit, yes, sir, quite a bit."

Big Bill and Anson were just beginning to nod their heads in agreement, when Charles stopped them.

"What do you expect of us in return?" he demanded of the old man.

"Oh, I leave it up to the boys."

"That ain't business," Charles reprimanded sharply. "You made the proposition. Now finish it."

"Well, it's this way—"

"You expect us to feed you all winter, eh?" Charles interrupted.

"No, siree, I don't. All I reckon is a passage to Klondike in your boat would be mighty square of you."

"You haven't an ounce of grub, old man. You'll starve to death when you get there."

"I've been feedin' some long time pretty successful," Old Tarwater replied, a whimsical light in his eyes. "I'm seventy, and ain't starved to death never yet."

"Will you sign a paper to the effect that you shift for yourself as soon as you get to Dawson?" the business one demanded.

"Oh, sure," was the response.

Again Charles checked his two partners' expressions of satisfaction with the arrangement.

"One other thing, old man. We're a party of four, and we all have a vote on questions like this. Young Liverpool is ahead with the main outfit. He's got a say so, and he isn't here to say it."

"What kind of a party might he be?" Tarwater inquired.

"He's a rough-neck sailor, and he's got a quick, bad temper."

"Some turbulent," Anson contributed.

"And the way he can cuss is simply God-awful," Big Bill testified.

"But he's square," Big Bill added.

Anson nodded heartily to this appraisal.

"Well, boys," Tarwater summed up, "I set out for Californy and I got there. And I'm going to get to Klondike. Ain't a thing can stop me, ain't a thing. I'm going to get three hundred thousand outa the ground, too. Ain't a thing can stop me, ain't a thing, because I just naturally need the money. I don't mind a bad temper so long's the boy is square. I'll take my chance, an' I'll work along with you till we catch up with him. Then, if he says no to the proposition, I reckon I'll lose. But somehow I just can't see 'm sayin' no, because that'd mean too close up to freeze-up and too late for me to find another chance like this. And, as I'm sure going to get to Klondike, it's just plumb impossible for him to say no."

Old John Tarwater became a striking figure on a trail unusually replete with striking figures. With thousands of men, each back-tripping half a ton of outfit, retracing every mile of the trail twenty times, all came to know him and to hail him as "Father Christmas." And, as he worked, ever he raised his chant with his age-falsetto voice. None of the three men he had joined could complain about his work. True, his joints were stiff—he admitted to a trifle of rheumatism. He moved slowly, and seemed to creak and crackle when he moved; but he kept on moving. Last into the blankets at night, he was first out in the morning, so that the other three had hot coffee before their one before-breakfast pack. And, between breakfast and dinner and between dinner and supper, he always managed to back-trip for several packs himself. Sixty pounds was the limit of his burden, however. He could manage seventy-five, but he could not keep it up. Once, he tried ninety, but collapsed on the trail and was seriously shaky for a couple of days afterward.

Work! On a trail where hard-working men learned for the first time what work was, no man worked harder in proportion to his strength than Old Tarwater. Driven desperately on by the near-thrust of winter, and lured madly on by the dream of gold, they worked to their last ounce of strength and fell by the way. Others, when failure made certain, blew out their brains. Some went mad, and still others, under the irk of the man-destroying strain, broke partnerships and dissolved life-time friendships with fellows just as good as themselves and just as strained and mad.

Work! Old Tarwater could shame them all, despite his creaking and crackling and the nasty hacking cough he had developed. Early and late, on trail or in camp beside the trail he was ever in evidence, ever busy at something, ever responsive to the hail of "Father Christmas." Weary back-trippers would rest their packs on a log or rock alongside of where he rested his, and would say: "Sing us that song of yourn, dad, about Forty-Nine." And, when he had wheezingly complied, they would arise under their loads, remark that it was real heartening, and hit the forward trail again.

"If ever a man worked his passage and earned it," Big Bill confided to his two partners, "that man's our old Skeezicks."

"You bet," Anson confirmed. "He's a valuable addition to the party, and I, for one, ain't at all disagreeable to the notion of making him a regular partner—"

"None of that!" Charles Crayton cut in. "When we get to Dawson we're quit of him—that's the agreement. We'd only have to bury him if we let him stay on with us. Besides, there's going to be a famine, and every ounce of grub'll count. Remember, we're feeding him out of our own supply all the way in. And if we run short in the pinch next year, you'll know the reason. Steamboats can't get up grub to Dawson till the middle of June, and that's nine months away."

"Well, you put as much money and outfit in as the rest of us," Big Bill conceded, "and you've a say according."

"And I'm going to have my say," Charles asserted with increasing irritability. "And it's lucky for you with your fool sentiments that you've got somebody to think ahead for you, else you'd all starve to death. I tell you that famine's coming. I've been studying the situation. Flour will be two dollars a pound, or ten, and no sellers. You mark my words."

Across the rubble-covered flats, up the dark canyon to Sheep Camp, past the over-hanging and ever-threatening glaciers to the Scales, and from the Scales up the steep pitches of ice-scoured rock where packers climbed with hands and feet, Old Tarwater camp-cooked and packed and sang. He blew across Chilcoot Pass, above timberline, in the first swirl of autumn snow. Those below, without firewood, on the bitter rim of Crater Lake, heard from the driving obscurity above them a weird voice chanting:

"Like Argus of the ancient times,

We leave this modern Greece,
Tum-tum, tum-tum, tum, tum, tum-tum,
To shear the Golden Fleece."

And out of the snow flurries they saw appear a tall, gaunt form, with whiskers of flying white that blended with the storm, bending under a sixty-pound pack of camp dunnage.

"Father Christmas!" was the hail. And then: "Three rousing cheers for Father Christmas!"

Two miles beyond Crater Lake lay Happy Camp—so named because here was found the uppermost fringe of the timber line, where men might warm themselves by fire again. Scarcely could it be called timber, for it was a dwarf rock-spruce that never raised its loftiest branches higher than a foot above the moss, and that twisted and grovelled like a pig-vegetable under the moss. Here, on the trail leading into Happy Camp, in the first sunshine of half a dozen days, Old Tarwater rested his pack against a huge boulder and caught his breath. Around this boulder the trail passed, laden men toiling slowly forward and men with empty pack-straps limping rapidly back for fresh loads. Twice Old Tarwater essayed to rise and go on, and each time, warned by his shakiness, sank back to recover more strength. From around the boulder he heard voices in greeting, recognized Charles Crayton's voice, and realized that at last they had met up with Young Liverpool. Quickly, Charles plunged into business, and Tarwater heard with great distinctness every word of Charles' unflattering description of him and the proposition to give him passage to Dawson.

"A dam fool proposition," was Liverpool's judgment, when Charles had concluded. "An old granddad of seventy! If he's on his last legs, why in hell did you hook up with him? If there's going to be a famine, and it looks like it, we need every ounce of grub for ourselves. We only out-fitted for four, not five."

"It's all right," Tarwater heard Charles assuring the other.

"Don't get excited. The old codger agreed to leave the final decision to you when we caught up with you. All you've got to do is put your foot down and say no."

"You mean it's up to me to turn the old one down, after your encouraging him and taking advantage of his work clear from Dyea here?"

"It's a hard trail, Liverpool, and only the men that are hard will get through," Charles strove to palliate.

"And I'm to do the dirty work?" Liverpool complained, while Tarwater's heart sank.

"That's just about the size of it," Charles said. "You've got the deciding."

Then old Tarwater's heart uprose again as the air was rent by a cyclone of profanity, from the midst of which crackled sentences like: —"Dirty skunks! . . . See you in hell first! . . . My mind's made up! . . . Hell's fire and corruption! . . . The old codger goes down the Yukon with us, stack on that, my hearty! . . . Hard? You don't know what hard is unless I show you! . . . I'll bust the whole outfit to hell and gone if any of you try to side-track him! . . . Just try to side-track him, that is all, and you'll think the Day of Judgment and all God's blastingness has hit the camp in one chunk!"

Such was the invigoratingness of Liverpool's flow of speech that, quite without consciousness of effort, the old man arose easily under his load and strode on toward Happy Camp.

From Happy Camp to Long Lake, from Long Lake to Deep Lake, and from Deep Lake up over the enormous hog-back and down to Linderman, the man-killing race against winter kept on. Men broke their hearts and backs and wept beside the trail in sheer exhaustion. But winter never faltered. The fall gales blew, and amid bitter soaking rains and ever-increasing snow flurries, Tarwater and the party to which he was attached piled the last of their outfit on the beach.

There was no rest. Across the lake, a mile above a roaring torrent, they located a patch of spruce and built their saw-pit. Here, by hand, with an inadequate whipsaw, they sawed the spruce-trunks into lumber. They worked night and day. Thrice, on the night-shift, underneath in the saw-pit, Old Tarwater fainted. By day he cooked as well, and, in the betweenwhiles, helped Anson in the building of the boat beside the torrent as the green planks came down.

The days grew shorter. The wind shifted into the north and blew unending gales. In the mornings the weary men crawled from their blankets and in their socks thawed out their frozen shoes by the fire Tarwater always had burning for them. Ever arose the increasing tale of famine on the Inside. The last grub steamboats up from Bering Sea were stalled by low water at the beginning of the Yukon Flats hundreds of miles north of Dawson. In fact, they lay at the old Hudson Bay Company's post at Fort Yukon inside the Arctic Circle. Flour in Dawson was up to two dollars a pound, but no one would sell. Bonanza and Eldorado Kings, with money to burn, were leaving for the Outside because they could buy no grub. Miners' Committees were confiscating all grub and putting the population on strict rations. A man who held out an ounce of grub was shot like a dog. A score had been so executed already.

And, under a strain which had broken so many younger men, Old Tarwater began to break. His cough had become terrible, and had not his exhausted comrades slept like the dead, he would have kept them awake nights. Also, he began to take chills, so that he dressed up to go to bed. When he had finished so dressing, not a rag of garment remained in his clothes bag. All he possessed was on his back and swathed around his gaunt old form.

"Gee!" said Big Bill. "If he puts all he's got on now, when it ain't lower than twenty above, what'll he do later on when it goes down to fifty and sixty below?"

They lined the rough-made boat down the mountain torrent, nearly losing it a dozen times, and rowed across the south end of Lake Linderman in the thick of a fall blizzard. Next morning they planned to load and start, squarely into the teeth of the north, on their perilous traverse of half a thousand miles of lakes and rapids and box canyons. But before he went to bed that night, Young Liverpool was out over the camp. He returned to find his whole party asleep. Rousing Tarwater, he talked with him in low tones.

"Listen, dad," he said.—"You've got a passage in our boat, and if ever a man earned a passage you have. But you know yourself you're pretty well along in years, and your health right now ain't exciting. If you go on with us you'll croak surer'n hell. —Now wait till I finish, dad. The price for a passage has jumped to five hundred dollars. I've been throwing my feet and I've hustled a passenger. He's an official of the Alaska Commercial and just has to get in. He's bid up to six hundred to go with me in our boat. Now the passage is yours. You sell it to him, poke the six hundred into your jeans, and pull South for California while the goin's good. You can be in Dyea in two days, and in California in a week more. What d'ye say?"

Tarwater coughed and shivered for a space, ere he could get freedom of breath for speech.

"Son," he said, "I just want to tell you one thing. I drove my four yoke of oxen across the Plains in Forty-nine and lost nary a one. I drove them plumb to Californy, and I freighted with them afterward out of Sutter's Fort to American Bar. Now I'm going to Klondike. Ain't nothing can stop me, ain't nothing at all. I'm going to ride that boat, with you at the steering sweep, clean to Klondike, and I'm going to shake three hundred thousand out of the moss-roots. That being so, it's contrary to reason and common sense for me to sell out my passage. But I thank you kindly, son, I thank you kindly."

The young sailor shot out his hand impulsively and gripped the old man's.

"By God, dad!" he cried. "You're sure going to go then. You're the real stuff." He looked with undisguised contempt across the sleepers to where Charles Crayton snored in his red beard. "They don't seem to make your kind any more, dad."

Into the north they fought their way, although old-timers, coming out, shook their heads and prophesied they would be frozen in on the lakes. That the freeze-up might come any day was patent, and delays of safety were no longer considered. For this reason, Liverpool decided to shoot the rapid stream connecting Linderman to Lake Bennett with the fully loaded boat. It was the custom to line the empty boats down and to portage the cargoes across. Even then many empty boats had been wrecked. But the time was past for such precaution.

"Climb out, dad," Liverpool commanded as he prepared to swing from the bank and enter the rapids.

Old Tarwater shook his white head.

"I'm sticking to the outfit," he declared. "It's the only way to get through. You see, son, I'm going to Klondike. If I stick by the boat, then the boat just naturally goes to Klondike, too. If I get out, then most likely you'll lose the boat."

"Well, there's no use in overloading," Charles announced, springing abruptly out on the bank as the boat cast off.

"Next time you wait for my orders!" Liverpool shouted ashore as the current gripped the boat. "And there won't be any more walking around rapids and losing time waiting to pick you up!"

What took them ten minutes by river, took Charles half an hour by land, and while they waited for him at the head of Lake Bennett they passed the time of day with several dilapidated old-timers on their way out. The famine news was graver than ever. The North-west Mounted Police, stationed at the foot of Lake Marsh where the gold-rushers entered

Canadian territory, were refusing to let a man past who did not carry with him seven hundred pounds of grub. In Dawson City a thousand men, with dog-teams, were waiting the freeze-up to come out over the ice. The trading companies could not fill their grub-contracts, and partners were cutting the cards to see which should go and which should stay and work the claims.

"That settles it," Charles announced, when he learned of the action of the mounted police on the boundary. "Old Man, you might as well start back now."

"Climb aboard!" Liverpool commanded. "We're going to Klondike, and old dad is going along."

A shift of gale to the south gave them a fair wind down Lake Bennett, before which they ran under a huge sail made by Liverpool. The heavy weight of outfit gave such ballast that he cracked on as a daring sailor should when moments counted. A shift of four points into the south-west, coming just at the right time as they entered upon Caribou Crossing, drove them down that connecting link to lakes Tagish and Marsh. In stormy sunset and twilight—they made the dangerous crossing of Great Windy Arm, wherein they beheld two other boat-loads of gold-rushers capsize and drown.

Charles was for beaching for the night, but Liverpool held on, steering down Tagish by the sound of the surf on the shoals and by the occasional shore-fires that advertised wrecked or timid argonauts. At four in the morning, he aroused Charles. Old Tarwater, shiveringly awake, heard Liverpool order Crayton aft beside him at the steering-sweep, and also heard the one-sided conversation.

"Just listen, friend Charles, and keep your own mouth shut," Liverpool began. "I want you to get one thing into your head and keep it there: OLD DAD'S GOING BY THE POLICE. UNDERSTAND? HE'S GOING BY. When they examine our outfit, old dad's got a fifth share in it, savvee? That'll put us all 'way under what we ought to have, but we can bluff it through. Now get this, and get it hard: THERE AIN'T GOING TO BE ANY FALL-DOWN ON THIS BLUFF—"

"If you think I'd give away on the old codger—" Charles began indignantly.

"You thought that," Liverpool checked him, "because I never mentioned any such thing. Now—get me and get me hard: I don't care what you've been thinking. It's what you're going to think. We'll make the police post some time this afternoon, and we've got to get ready to pull the bluff without a hitch, and a word to the wise is plenty."

"If you think I've got it in my mind—" Charles began again.

"Look here," Liverpool shut him off. "I don't know what's in your mind. I don't want to know. I want you to know what's in my mind. If there's any slip-up, if old dad gets turned back by the police, I'm going to pick out the first quiet bit of landscape and take you ashore on it. And then I'm going to beat you up to the Queen's taste. Get me, and get me hard. It ain't going to be any half-way beating, but a real, two-legged, two-fisted, he-man beating. I don't expect I'll kill you, but I'll come damn near to half-killing you."

"But what can I do?" Charles almost whimpered.

"Just one thing," was Liverpool's final word. "You just pray. You pray so hard that old dad gets by the police that he does get by. That's all. Go back to your blankets."

Before they gained Lake Le Barge, the land was sheeted with snow that would not melt for half a year. Nor could they lay their boat at will against the bank, for the rim-ice was already forming. Inside the mouth of the river, just ere it entered Lake Le Barge, they found a hundred storm-bound boats of the argonauts. Out of the north, across the full sweep of the great lake, blew an unending snow gale. Three mornings they put out and fought it and the cresting seas it drove that turned to ice as they fell in-board. While the others broke their hearts at the oars, Old Tarwater managed to keep up just sufficient circulation to survive by chopping ice and throwing it overboard.

Each day for three days, beaten to helplessness, they turned tail on the battle and ran back into the sheltering river. By the fourth day, the hundred boats had increased to three hundred, and the two thousand argonauts on board knew that the great gale heralded the freeze-up of Le Barge. Beyond, the rapid rivers would continue to run for days, but unless they got beyond, and immediately, they were doomed to be frozen in for six months to come.

"This day we go through," Liverpool announced. "We turn back for nothing. And those of us that dies at the oars will live again and go on pulling."

And they went through, winning half the length of the lake by nightfall and pulling on through all the night hours as the wind went down, falling asleep at the oars and being rapped awake by Liverpool, toiling on through an age-long nightmare while the stars came out and the surface of the lake turned to the unruffledness of a sheet of paper and froze skin-ice that tinkled like broken glass as their oar-blades shattered it.

As day broke clear and cold, they entered the river, with behind them a sea of ice. Liverpool examined his aged passenger and found him helpless and almost gone. When he rounded the boat to against the rim-ice to build a fire and warm up Tarwater inside and out, Charles protested against such loss of time.

"This ain't business, so don't you come horning in," Liverpool informed him. "I'm running the boat trip. So you just climb out and chop firewood, and plenty of it. I'll take care of dad. You, Anson, make a fire on the bank. And you, Bill, set up the Yukon stove in the boat. Old dad ain't as young as the rest of

Jack London

us, and for the rest of this voyage he's going to have a fire on board to sit by."

All of which came to pass; and the boat, in the grip of the current, like a river steamer with smoke rising from the two joints of stove-pipe, grounded on shoals, hung up on split currents, and charged rapids and canyons, as it drove deeper into the Northland winter. The Big and Little Salmon rivers were throwing mush-ice into the main river as they passed, and, below the riffles, anchor-ice arose from the river bottom and coated the surface with crystal scum. Night and day the rim-ice grew, till, in quiet places, it extended out a hundred yards from shore. And Old Tarwater, with all his clothes on, sat by the stove and kept the fire going. Night and day, not daring to stop for fear of the imminent freeze-up, they dared to run, an increasing mushiness of ice running with them.

"What ho, old hearty?" Liverpool would call out at times.

"Cheer O," Old Tarwater had learned to respond.

"What can I ever do for you, son, in payment?" Tarwater, stoking the fire, would sometimes ask Liverpool, beating now one released hand and now the other as he fought for circulation where he steered in the freezing stern-sheets.

"Just break out that regular song of yours, old Forty-Niner," was the invariable reply.

And Tarwater would lift his voice in the cackling chant, as he lifted it at the end, when the boat swung in through driving cake-ice and moored to the Dawson City bank, and all waterfront Dawson pricked its ears to hear the triumphant paean:

Like Argus of the ancient times,
We leave this modern Greece,
Tum-tum, tum-tum, tum, tum, tum-tum,
To shear the Golden Fleece,

Charles did it, but he did it so discreetly that none of his party, least of all the sailor, ever learned of it. He saw two great open barges being filled up with men, and, on inquiry, learned that these were grubless ones being rounded up and sent down the Yukon by the Committee of Safety. The barges were to be towed by the last little steamboat in Dawson, and the hope was that Fort Yukon, where lay the stranded steamboats, would be gained before the river froze. At any rate, no matter what happened to them, Dawson would be relieved of their grub-consuming presence. So to the Committee of Safety Charles went, privily to drop a flea in its ear concerning Tarwater's grubless, moneyless, and aged condition. Tarwater was one of the last gathered in, and when Young Liverpool returned to the boat, from the bank he saw the barges in a run of cake-ice, disappearing around the bend below Moose-hide Mountain.

Running in cake-ice all the way, and several times escaping jams in the Yukon Flats, the barges made their hundreds of miles of progress farther into the north and froze up cheek by jowl with the grub-fleet. Here, inside the Arctic Circle, Old Tarwater settled down to pass the long winter. Several hours' work a day, chopping firewood for the steamboat companies, sufficed to keep him in food. For the rest of the time there was nothing to do but hibernate in his log cabin.

Warmth, rest, and plenty to eat, cured his hacking cough and put him in as good physical condition as was possible for his advanced years. But, even before Christmas, the lack of fresh vegetables caused scurvy to break out, and disappointed adventurer after disappointed adventurer took to his bunk in abject surrender to this culminating misfortune. Not so Tarwater. Even before the first symptoms appeared on him, he was putting into practice his one prescription, namely, exercise. From the junk of the old trading post he resurrected a number of rusty traps, and from one of the steamboat captains he borrowed a rifle.

Thus equipped, he ceased from wood-chopping, and began to make more than a mere living. Nor was he downhearted when the scurvy broke out on his own body. Ever he ran his trap-lines and sang his ancient chant. Nor could the pessimist shake his surety of the three hundred thousand of Alaskan gold he as going to shake out of the moss-roots.

"But this ain't gold-country," they told him.

"Gold is where you find it, son, as I should know who was mining before you was born, 'way back in Forty-Nine," was his reply. "What was Bonanza Creek but a moose-pasture? No miner'd look at it; yet they washed five-hundred-dollar pans and took out fifty million dollars. Eldorado was just as bad. For all you know, right under this here cabin, or right over the next hill, is millions just waiting for a lucky one like me to come and shake it out."

At the end of January came his disaster. Some powerful animal that he decided was a bob-cat, managing to get caught in one of his smaller traps, dragged it away. A heavy snow-fall put a stop midway to his pursuit, losing the trail for him and losing himself. There were but several hours of daylight each day between the twenty hours of intervening darkness, and his efforts in the grey light and continually falling snow succeeded only in losing him more thoroughly. Fortunately, when winter snow falls in the Northland the thermometer invariably rises; so, instead of the customary forty and fifty and even sixty degrees below zero, the temperature remained fifteen below. Also, he was warmly clad and had a full matchbox. Further to mitigate his predicament, on the fifth day he killed a wounded moose that weighed over half a ton. Making his camp beside it on a spruce-bottom, he was prepared to last out the winter, unless a searching party found him or his scurvy grew worse.

But at the end of two weeks there had been no sign of search, while his scurvy had undeniably grown worse. Against his fire, banked from outer cold by a shelter-wall of spruce-boughs, he crouched long hours in sleep and long hours in waking. But the waking hours grew less, becoming semi-waking or half-dreaming hours as the process of hibernation worked their way with him. Slowly the sparkle point of consciousness and identity that was John Tarwater sank, deeper and deeper, into the profounds of his being that had been compounded ere man was man, and while he was becoming man, when he, first of all animals, regarded himself with an introspective eye and laid the beginnings of morality in foundations of nightmare peopled by the monsters of his own ethic- thwarted desires.

Like a man in fever, waking to intervals of consciousness, so Old Tarwater awoke, cooked his moose-meat, and fed the fire; but more and more time he spent in his torpor, unaware of what was day-dream and what was sleep-dream in the content of his unconsciousness. And here, in the unforgetable crypts of man's unwritten history, unthinkable and unrealizable, like passages of nightmare or impossible adventures of lunacy, he encountered the monsters created of man's first morality that ever since have vexed him into the spinning of fantasies to elude them or do battle with them.

In short, weighted by his seventy years, in the vast and silent loneliness of the North, Old Tarwater, as in the delirium of drug or anaesthetic, recovered within himself, the infantile mind of the child-man of the early world. It was in the dusk of Death's fluttery wings that Tarwater thus crouched, and, like his remote forebear, the child-man, went to myth-making, and sun-heroizing, himself hero-maker and the hero in quest of the immemorable treasure difficult of attainment.

Either must he attain the treasure—for so ran the inexorable logic of the shadow-land of the unconscious—or else sink into the all-devouring sea, the blackness eater of the light that swallowed to extinction the sun each night . . . the sun that arose ever in rebirth next morning in the east, and that had become to man man's first symbol of immortality through rebirth. All this, in the deeps of his unconsciousness (the shadowy western land of descending light), was the near dusk of Death down into which he slowly ebbed.

But how to escape this monster of the dark that from within

him slowly swallowed him? Too deep-sunk was he to dream of escape or feel the prod of desire to escape. For him reality had ceased. Nor from within the darkened chamber of himself could reality recrudesce. His years were too heavy upon him, the debility of disease and the lethargy and torpor of the silence and the cold were too profound. Only from without could reality impact upon him and reawake within him an awareness of reality. Otherwise he would ooze down through the shadow-realm of the unconscious into the all-darkness of extinction.

But it came, the smash of reality from without, crashing upon his ear drums in a loud, explosive snort. For twenty days, in a temperature that had never risen above fifty below, no breath of wind had blown movement, no slightest sound had broken the silence. Like the smoker on the opium couch refocusing his eyes from the spacious walls of dream to the narrow confines of the mean little room, so Old Tarwater stared vague-eyed before him across his dying fire, at a huge moose that stared at him in startlement, dragging a wounded leg, manifesting all signs of extreme exhaustion; it, too, had been straying blindly in the shadow-land, and had wakened to reality only just ere it stepped into Tarwater's fire.

He feebly slipped the large fur mitten lined with thickness of wool from his right hand. Upon trial he found the trigger finger too numb for movement. Carefully, slowly, through long minutes, he worked the bare hand inside his blankets, up under his fur parka, through the chest openings of his shirts, and into the slightly warm hollow of his left arm-pit. Long minutes passed ere the finger could move, when, with equal slowness of caution, he gathered his rifle to his shoulder and drew bead upon the great animal across the fire.

At the shot, of the two shadow-wanderers, the one reeled downward to the dark and the other reeled upward to the light, swaying drunkenly on his scurvy-ravaged legs, shivering with nervousness and cold, rubbing swimming eyes with shaking fingers, and staring at the real world all about him that had returned to him with such sickening suddenness. He shook himself together, and realized that for long, how long he did not know, he had bedded in the arms of Death. He spat, with definite intention, heard the spittle crackle in the frost, and judged it must be below and far below sixty below. In truth, that day at Fort Yukon, the spirit thermometer registered seventy-five degrees below zero, which, since freezing-point is thirty-two above, was equivalent to one hundred and seven degrees of frost.

Slowly Tarwater's brain reasoned to action. Here, in the vast alone, dwelt Death. Here had come two wounded moose. With the clearing of the sky after the great cold came on, he had located his bearings, and he knew that both wounded moose had trailed to him from the east. Therefore, in the east, were men—whites or Indians he could not tell, but at any rate men who might stand by him in his need and help moor him to reality above the sea of dark.

He moved slowly, but he moved in reality, girding himself with rifle, ammunition, matches, and a pack of twenty pounds of moose-meat. Then, an Argus rejuvenated, albeit lame of both legs and tottery, he turned his back on the perilous west and limped into the sun-arising, re-birthing east. . . .

Days later—how many days later he was never to know—dreaming dreams and seeing visions, cackling his old gold-chant of Forty-Nine, like one drowning and swimming feebly to keep his consciousness above the engulfing dark, he came out upon the snow-slope to a canyon and saw below smoke rising and men who ceased from work to gaze at him. He tottered down the hill to them, still singing; and when he ceased from lack of breath they called him variously: Santa Claus, Old Christmas, Whiskers, the Last of the Mohicans, and Father Christmas. And when he stood among them he stood very still, without speech, while great tears welled out of his eyes. He cried silently, a long time, till, as if suddenly bethinking himself, he sat down in the snow with much creaking and crackling of his joints, and from this low vantage point toppled sidewise and fainted calmly and easily away.

In less than a week Old Tarwater was up and limping about the housework of the cabin, cooking and dish-washing for the five men of the creek. Genuine sourdoughs (pioneers) they were, tough and hard-bitten, who had been buried so deeply inside the Circle that they did not know there was a Klondike Strike. The news he brought them was their first word of it. They lived on an almost straight-meat diet of moose, caribou, and smoked salmon, eked out with wild berries and somewhat succulent wild roots they had stocked up with in the summer. They had forgotten the taste of coffee, made fire with a burning glass, carried live fire-sticks with them wherever they travelled, and in their pipes smoked dry leaves that bit the tongue and were pungent to the nostrils.

Three years before, they had prospected from the head-reaches of the Koyokuk northward and clear across to the mouth of the Mackenzie on the Arctic Ocean. Here, on the whaleships, they had beheld their last white men and equipped themselves with the last white man's grub, consisting principally of salt and smoking tobacco. Striking south and west on the long traverse to the junction of the Yukon and Porcupine at Fort Yukon, they had found gold on this creek and remained over to work the ground.

They hailed the advent of Tarwater with joy, never tired of listening to his tales of Forty-Nine, and rechristened him Old Hero. Also, with tea made from spruce needles, with concoctions brewed from the inner willow bark, and with sour and bitter roots and bulbs from the ground, they dosed his scurvy out of him, so that he ceased limping and began to lay on flesh over his bony framework. Further, they saw no reason at all why he should not gather a rich treasure of gold from the ground.

"Don't know about all of three hundred thousand," they told him one morning, at breakfast, ere they departed to their work, "but how'd a hundred thousand do, Old Hero? That's what we figure a claim is worth, the ground being badly spotted, and we've already staked your location notices."

"Well, boys," Old Tarwater answered, "and thanking you kindly, all I can say is that a hundred thousand will do nicely, and very nicely, for a starter. Of course, I ain't goin' to stop till I get the full three hundred thousand. That's what I come into the country for."

They laughed and applauded his ambition and reckoned they'd have to hunt a richer creek for him. And Old Hero reckoned that as the spring came on and he grew spryer, he'd have to get out and do a little snooping around himself.

"For all anybody knows," he said, pointing to a hillside across the creek bottom, "the moss under the snow there may be plumb rooted in nugget gold."

He said no more, but as the sun rose higher and the days grew longer and warmer, he gazed often across the creek at the definite bench-formation half way up the hill. And, one day, when the thaw was in full swing, he crossed the stream and climbed to the bench. Exposed patches of ground had already thawed an inch deep. On one such patch he stopped, gathered a bunch of moss in his big gnarled hands, and ripped it out by the roots. The sun smouldered on dully glistening yellow. He shook the handful of moss, and coarse nuggets, like gravel, fell to the ground. It was the Golden Fleece ready for the shearing.

Not entirely unremembered in Alaskan annals is the summer stampede of 1898 from Fort Yukon to the bench diggings of Tarwater Hill. And when Tarwater sold his holdings to the Bowdie interests for a sheer half-million and faced for California, he rode a mule over a new-cut trail, with convenient road houses along the way, clear to the steamboat landing at Fort Yukon.

At the first meal on the ocean-going steamship out of St. Michaels, a waiter, greyish-haired, pain-ravaged of face, scurvy-twisted of body, served him. Old Tarwater was compelled to look him over twice in order to make certain he was Charles Crayton.

"Got it bad, eh, son?" Tarwater queried.

"Just my luck," the other complained, after recognition and greeting. "Only one of the party that the scurvy attacked. I've been through hell. The other three are all at work and healthy, getting grub-stake to prospect up White River this winter. Anson's earning twenty-five a day at carpentering, Liverpool getting twenty logging for the saw-mill, and Big Bill's getting forty a day as chief sawyer. I tried my best, and if it hadn't been for scurvy . . ."

"Sure, son, you done your best, which ain't much, you being naturally irritable and hard from too much business. Now I'll tell you what. You ain't fit to work crippled up this way. I'll pay your passage with the captain in kind remembrance of the voyage you gave me, and you can lay up and take it easy the rest of the trip. And what are your circumstances when you land at San Francisco?"

Charles Crayton shrugged his shoulders.

"Tell you what," Tarwater continued. "There's work on the ranch for you till you can start business again."

"I could manage your business for you—" Charles began eagerly.

"No, siree," Tarwater declared emphatically. "But there's always post-holes to dig, and cordwood to chop, and the climate's fine . . . "

Tarwater arrived home a true prodigal grandfather for whom the fatted calf was killed and ready. But first, ere he sat down at table, he must stroll out and around. And sons and daughters of his flesh and of the law needs must go with him fulsomely eating out of the gnarled old hand that had half a million to disburse. He led the way, and no opinion he slyly uttered was preposterous or impossible enough to draw dissent from his following. Pausing by the ruined water wheel which he had built from the standing timber, his face beamed as he gazed across the stretches of Tarwater Valley, and on and up the far heights to the summit of Tarwater Mountain—now all his again.

A thought came to him that made him avert his face and blow his nose in order to hide the twinkle in his eyes. Still attended by the entire family, he strolled on to the dilapidated barn. He picked up an age-weathered single-tree from the ground.

"William," he said. "Remember that little conversation we had just before I started to Klondike? Sure, William, you remember. You told me I was crazy. And I said my father'd have walloped the tar out of me with a single-tree if I'd spoke to him that way."

"Aw, but that was only foolin'," William temporized.

William was a grizzled man of forty-five, and his wife and grown sons stood in the group, curiously watching Grandfather Tarwater take off his coat and hand it to Mary to hold.

"William—come here," he commanded imperatively.

No matter how reluctantly, William came.

"Just a taste, William, son, of what my father give me often enough," Old Tarwater crooned, as he laid on his son's back and shoulders with the single-tree. "Observe, I ain't hitting you on the head. My father had a gosh-wollickin' temper and never drew the line at heads when he went after tar.—Don't jerk your elbows back that way! You're likely to get a crack on one by accident. And just tell me one thing, William, son: is there nary notion in your head that I'm crazy?"

"No!" William yelped out in pain, as he danced about. "You ain't crazy, father of course you ain't crazy!"

"You said it," Old Tarwater remarked sententiously, tossing the single-tree aside and starting to struggle into his coat.

"Now let's all go in and eat."

Glen Ellen, California, September 14, 1916.

THE PRINCESS

A fire burned cheerfully in the jungle camp, and beside the fire lolled a cheerful-seeming though horrible-appearing man. This was a hobo jungle, pitched in a thin strip of woods that lay between a railroad embankment and the bank of a river. But no hobo was the man. So deep-sunk was he in the social abyss that a proper hobo would not sit by the same fire with him. A gay-cat, who is an ignorant new-comer on the "Road," might sit with such as he, but only long enough to learn better. Even low down bindle-stiffs and stew-bums, after a once-over, would have passed this man by. A genuine hobo, a couple of punks, or a bunch of tender-yeared road-kids might have gone through his rags for any stray pennies or nickels and kicked him out into the darkness. Even an alki-stiff would have reckoned himself immeasurably superior.

For this man was that hybrid of tramp-land, an alki-stiff that has degenerated into a stew-bum, with so little self-respect that he will never "boil-up," and with so little pride that he will eat out of a garbage can. He was truly horrible-appearing. He might have been sixty years of age; he might have been ninety. His garments might have been discarded by a rag-picker. Beside him, an unrolled bundle showed itself as consisting of a ragged overcoat and containing an empty and smoke-blackened tomato can, an empty and battered condensed milk can, some dog-meat partly wrapped in brown paper and evidently begged from some butcher-shop, a carrot that had been run over in the street by a wagon-wheel, three greenish-cankered and decayed potatoes, and a sugar-bun with a mouthful bitten from it and rescued from the gutter, as was made patent by the gutter-filth that still encrusted it.

A prodigious growth of whiskers, greyish-dirty and untrimmed for years, sprouted from his face. This hirsute growth should have been white, but the season was summer and it had not been exposed to a rain-shower for some time. What was visible of the face looked as if at some period it had stopped a hand-grenade. The nose was so variously malformed in its healed brokenness that there was no bridge, while one nostril, the size of a pea, opened downward, and the other, the size of a robin's egg, tilted upward to the sky. One eye, of normal size, dim-brown and misty, bulged to the verge of popping out, and as if from senility wept copiously and continuously. The other eye, scarcely larger than a squirrel's and as uncannily bright, twisted up obliquely into the hairy scar of a bone-crushed eyebrow. And he had but one arm.

Yet was he cheerful. On his face, in mild degree, was depicted sensuous pleasure as he lethargically scratched his ribs with his one hand. He pawed over his food-scraps, debated, then drew a twelve-ounce druggist bottle from his inside coat-pocket. The bottle was full of a colourless liquid, the contemplation of which made his little eye burn brighter and quickened his movements. Picking up the tomato can, he arose, went down the short path to the river, and returned with the can filled with not-nice river water. In the condensed milk can he mixed one part of water with two parts of fluid from the bottle. This colourless fluid was druggist's alcohol, and as such is known in tramp-land as "alki."

Slow footsteps, coming down the side of the railroad embankment, alarmed him ere he could drink. Placing the can carefully upon the ground between his legs, he covered it with his hat and waited anxiously whatever impended.

Out of the darkness emerged a man as filthy ragged as he. The new-comer, who might have been fifty, and might have been sixty, was grotesquely fat. He bulged everywhere. He was composed of bulges. His bulbous nose was the size and shape of a turnip. His eyelids bulged and his blue eyes bulged in competition with them. In many places the seams of his garments had parted across the bulges of body. His calves grew into his feet, for the broken elastic sides of his Congress gaiters were swelled full with the fat of him. One arm only he sported, from the shoulder of which was suspended a small and tattered bundle with the mud caked dry on the outer covering from the last place he had pitched his doss. He advanced with tentative caution, made sure of the harmlessness of the man beside the fire, and joined him.

"Hello, grandpa," the new-comer greeted, then paused to stare at the other's flaring, sky-open nostril. "Say, Whiskers, how'd ye keep the night dew out of that nose o' yourn?"

Whiskers growled an incoherence deep in his throat and spat into the fire in token that he was not pleased by the question.

"For the love of Mike," the fat man chuckled, "if you got caught out in a rainstorm without an umbrella you'd sure drown, wouldn't you?"

"Can it, Fatty, can it," Whiskers muttered wearily. "They ain't nothin' new in that line of chatter. Even the bulls hand it out to me."

"But you can still drink, I hope"; Fatty at the same time mollified and invited, with his one hand deftly pulling the slip-knots that fastened his bundle.

From within the bundle he brought to light a twelve-ounce bottle of alki. Footsteps coming down the embankment alarmed him, and he hid the bottle under his hat on the ground between his legs.

But the next comer proved to be not merely one of their own ilk, but likewise to have only one arm. So forbidding of aspect was he that greetings consisted of no more than grunts.

Huge-boned, tall, gaunt to cadaverousness, his face a dirty death's head, he was as repellent a nightmare of old age as ever Doré imagined. His toothless, thin-lipped mouth was a cruel and bitter slash under a great curved nose that almost met the chin and that was like a buzzard's beak. His one hand, lean and crooked, was a talon. The beady grey eyes, unblinking and unwavering, were bitter as death, as bleak as absolute zero and as merciless. His presence was a chill, and Whiskers and Fatty instinctively drew together for protection against the unguessed threat of him. Watching his chance, privily, Whiskers snuggled a chunk of rock several pounds in weigh close to his hand if need for action should arise. Fatty duplicated the performance.

Then both sat licking their lips, guiltily embarrassed, while the unblinking eyes of the terrible one bored into them, now into one, now into another, and then down at the rock-chunks of their preparedness.

"Huh!" sneered the terrible one, with such dreadfulness of menace as to cause Whiskers and Fatty involuntarily to close their hands down on their cave-man's weapons.

"Huh!" the other repeated, reaching his one talon into his side coat pocket with swift definiteness. "A hell of a chance you two cheap bums 'd have with me."

The talon emerged, clutching ready for action a six-pound iron quoit.

"We ain't lookin' for trouble, Slim," Fatty quavered.

"Who in hell are you to call me 'Slim'?" came the snarling answer.

"Me? I'm just Fatty, an' seein' 's I never seen you before—"

"An' I suppose that's Whiskers, there, with the gay an' festive lamp tan-going into his eyebrow an' the God-forgive-us nose joy-riding all over his mug?"

"It'll do, it'll do," Whiskers muttered uncomfortably. "One monica's as good as another, I find, at my time of life. And everybody hands it out to me anyway. And I need an umbrella when it rains to keep from getting drowned, an' all the rest of it."

"I ain't used to company—don't like it," Slim growled. "So if you guys want to stick around, mind your step, that's all, mind your step."

He fished from his pocket a cigar stump, self-evidently shot from the gutter, and prepared to put it in his mouth to chew. Then he changed his mind, glared at his companions savagely, and unrolled his bundle. Appeared in his hand a druggist's bottle of alki.

"Well," he snarled, "I suppose I gotta give you cheap skates a drink when I ain't got more'n enough for a good petrification for myself."

Almost a softening flicker of light was imminent in his withered face as he beheld the others proudly lift their hats and exhibit their own supplies.

"Here's some water for the mixin's," Whiskers said, proffering his tomato-can of river slush. "Stockyards just above," he added apologetically. "But they say—"

"Huh!" Slim snapped short, mixing the drink. "I've drunk worse'n stockyards in my time."

Yet when all was ready, cans of alki in their solitary hands, the three things that had once been men hesitated, as if of old habit, and next betrayed shame as if at self-exposure.

Whiskers was the first to brazen it.

"I've sat in at many a finer drinking," he bragged.

"With the pewter," Slim sneered.

"With the silver," Whiskers corrected.

Slim turned a scorching eye-interrogation on Fatty.

Fatty nodded.

"Beneath the salt," said Slim.

"Above it," came Fatty's correction. "I was born above it, and I've never travelled second class. First or steerage, but no intermediate in mine."

"Yourself?" Whiskers queried of Slim.

"In broken glass to the Queen, God bless her," Slim answered, solemnly, without snarl or sneer.

"In the pantry?" Fatty insinuated.

Simultaneously Slim reached for his quoit, and Whiskers and Fatty for their rocks.

"Now don't let's get feverish," Fatty said, dropping his own weapon. "We aren't scum. We're gentlemen. Let's drink like gentlemen."

"Let it be a real drinking," Whiskers approved.

"Let's get petrified," Slim agreed. "Many a distillery's flowed under the bridge since we were gentlemen; but let's forget the long road we've travelled since, and hit our doss in the good old fashion in which every gentleman went to bed when we were young."

"My father done it—did it," Fatty concurred and corrected, as old recollections exploded long-sealed brain-cells of connotation and correct usage.

The other two nodded a descent from similar fathers, and elevated their tin cans of alcohol.

By the time each had finished his own bottle and from his rags fished forth a second one, their brains were well-mellowed and a-glow, although they had not got around to telling their real names. But their English had improved. They spoke it correctly, while the argo of tramp-land ceased from their lips.

"It's my constitution," Whiskers was explaining. "Very few men could go through what I have and live to tell the tale. And I never took any care of myself. If what the moralists and the physiologists say were true, I'd have been dead long ago. And it's the same with you two. Look at us, at our advanced years, carousing as the young ones don't dare, sleeping out in the open on the ground, never sheltered from frost nor rain nor storm, never afraid of pneumonia or rheumatism that would put half the young ones on their backs in hospital."

He broke off to mix another drink, and Fatty took up the tale.

"And we've had our fun," he boasted, "and speaking of sweethearts and all," he cribbed from Kipling, "We've rogued and we've ranged—"

"In our time," Slim completed the crib for him.

"I should say so, I should say so," Fatty confirmed. "And been loved by princesses—at least I have."

"Go on and tell us about it," Whiskers urged. "The night's young, and why shouldn't we remember back to the roofs of kings?"

Nothing loth, Fatty cleared his throat for the recital and cast about in his mind for the best way to begin.

"It must be known that I came of good family. Percival Delaney, let us say, yes, let us say Percival Delaney, was not unknown at Oxford once upon a time—not for scholarship, I am frank to admit; but the gay young dogs of that day, if any be yet alive, would remember him—"

"My people came over with the Conqueror," Whiskers interrupted, extending his hand to Fatty's in acknowledgment of the introduction.

"What name?" Fatty queried. "I did not seem quite to catch it."

"Delarouse, Chauncey Delarouse. The name will serve as well as any."

Both completed the handshake and glanced to Slim.

"Oh, well, while we're about it . . . " Fatty urged.

"Bruce Cadogan Cavendish," Slim growled morosely. "Go on, Percival, with your princesses and the roofs of kings."

"Oh, I was a rare young devil," Percival obliged, "after I played ducks and drakes at home and sported out over the world. And I was some figure of a man before I lost my shape—polo, steeple-chasing, boxing. I won medals at buckjumping in Australia, and I held more than several swimming records from the quarter of a mile up. Women turned their heads to look when I went by. The women! God bless them!"

And Fatty, alias Percival Delaney, a grotesque of manhood, put his bulgy hand to his puffed lips and kissed audibly into the starry vault of the sky.

"And the Princess!" he resumed, with another kiss to the stars. "She was as fine a figure of a woman as I was a man, as high-spirited and courageous, as reckless and dare-devilish. Lord, Lord, in the water she was a mermaid, a sea-goddess. And when it came to blood, beside her I was parvenu. Her royal line traced back into the mists of antiquity.

"She was not a daughter of a fair-skinned folk. Tawny golden was she, with golden-brown eyes, and her hair that fell to her knees was blue-black and straight, with just the curly tendrilly tendency that gives to woman's hair its charm. Oh, there were no kinks in it, any more than were there kinks in the hair of her entire genealogy. For she was Polynesian, glowing, golden, lovely and lovable, royal Polynesian."

Again he paused to kiss his hand to the memory of her, and Slim, alias Bruce Cadogan Cavendish, took advantage to interject:

"Huh! Maybe you didn't shine in scholarship, but at least you gleaned a vocabulary out of Oxford."

"And in the South Seas garnered a better vocabulary from the lexicon of Love," Percival was quick on the uptake.

"It was the island of Talofa," he went on, "meaning love, the Isle of Love, and it was her island. Her father, the king, an old man, sat on his mats with paralysed knees and drank squareface gin all day and most of the night, out of grief, sheer grief. She, my princess, was the only issue, her brother having been lost in their double canoe in a hurricane while coming up from a voyage to Samoa. And among the Polynesians the royal women have equal right with the men to rule. In fact, they trace their genealogies always by the female line."

To this both Chauncey Delarouse and Bruce Cadogan Cavendish nodded prompt affirmation.

"Ah," said Percival, "I perceive you both know the South Seas, wherefore, without undue expenditure of verbiage on my part, I am assured that you will appreciate the charm of my princess, the Princess Tui-nui of Talofa, the Princess of the Isle of Love."

He kissed his hand to her, sipped from his condensed milk can a man-size drink of druggist's alcohol, and to her again kissed her hand.

"But she was coy, and ever she fluttered near to me but never near enough. When my arm went out to her to girdle her, presto, she was not there. I knew, as never before, nor since, the thousand dear and delightful anguishes of love frustrated but ever resilient and beckoned on by the very goddess of love."

"Some vocabulary," Bruce Cadogan Cavendish muttered in aside to Chauncey Delarouse. But Percival Delaney was not to be deterred. He kissed his pudgy hand aloft into the night and held warmly on.

"No fond agonies of rapture deferred that were not lavished upon me by my dear Princess, herself ever a luring delight of promise flitting just beyond my reach. Every sweet lover's inferno unguessed of by Dante she led me through. Ah! Those swooning tropic nights, under our palm trees, the distant surf a languorous murmur as from some vast sea shell of mystery, when she, my Princess, all but melted to my yearning, and with her laughter, that was as silver strings by buds and blossoms smitten, all but made lunacy of my lover's ardency.

"It was by my wrestling with the champions of Talofa that I first interested her. It was by my prowess at swimming that I awoke her. And it was by a certain swimming deed that I won from her more than coquettish smiles and shy timidities of feigned retreat.

"We were squidding that day, out on the reef—you know how, undoubtedly, diving down the face of the wall of the reef, five fathoms, ten fathoms, any depth within reason, and shoving our squid-sticks into the likely holes and crannies of the coral where squid might be lairing. With the squid-stick, bluntly sharp at both ends, perhaps a foot long, and held crosswise in the hand, the trick was to gouge any lazying squid until he closed his tentacles around fist, stick and arm.—Then you had him, and came to the surface with him, and hit him in the head which is in the centre of him, and peeled him off into the waiting canoe. . . . And to think I used to do that!"

Percival Delaney paused a moment, a glimmer of awe on his rotund face, as he contemplated the mighty picture of his youth.

"Why, I've pulled out a squid with tentacles eight feet long, and done it under fifty feet of water. I could stay down four minutes. I've gone down, with a coral-rock to sink me, in a hundred and ten feet to clear a fouled anchor. And I could back-dive with a once-over and go in feet-first from eighty feet above the surface—"

"Quit it, delete it, cease it," Chauncey Delarouse admonished testily. "Tell of the Princess. That's what makes old blood leap again. Almost can I see her. Was she wonderful?"

Percival Delaney kissed unutterable affirmation.

"I have said she was a mermaid. She was. I know she swam thirty-six hours before being rescued, after her schooner was capsized in a double-squall. I have seen her do ninety feet and bring up pearl shell in each hand. She was wonderful. As a woman she was ravishing, sublime. I have said she was a sea-goddess. She was. Oh, for a Phidias or a Praxiteles to have made the wonder of her body immortal!

"And that day, out for squid on the reef, I was almost sick for her. Mad—I know I was mad for her. We would step over the side from the big canoe, and swim down, side by side, into the delicious depths of cool and colour, and she would look at me, as we swam, and with her eyes tantalize me to further madness. And at last, down, far down, I lost myself and reached for her. She eluded me like the mermaid she was, and I saw the laughter on her face as she fled. She fled deeper, and I knew I had her for I was between her and the surface; but in the muck coral sand of the bottom she made a churning with her squid stick. It was the old trick to escape a shark. And she worked it on me, rolling the water so that I could not see her. And when I came up, she was there ahead of me, clinging to the side of the canoe and laughing.

"Almost I would not be denied. But not for nothing was she a princess. She rested her hand on my arm and compelled me to listen. We should play a game, she said, enter into a competition for which should get the more squid, the biggest squid, and the smallest squid. Since the wagers were kisses, you can well imagine I went down on the first next dive with soul aflame.

"I got no squid. Never again in all my life have I dived for squid. Perhaps we were five fathoms down and exploring the face of the reefwall for lurking places of our prey, when it happened. I had found a likely lair and just proved it empty, when I felt or sensed the nearness of something inimical. I turned. There it was, alongside of me, and no mere fish-shark. Fully a dozen feet in length, with the unmistakable phosphorescent cat's eye gleaming like a drowning star, I knew it for what it was, a tiger shark.

"Not ten feet to the right, probing a coral fissure with her squid stick, was the Princess, and the tiger shark was heading directly for her. My totality of thought was precipitated to consciousness in a single all-embracing flash. The man-eater must be deflected from her, and what was I, except a mad lover who would gladly fight and die, or more gladly fight and live, for his beloved? Remember, she was the woman wonderful, and I was aflame for her.

"Knowing fully the peril of my act, I thrust the blunt-sharp end of my squid-stick into the side of the shark, much as one would attract a passing acquaintance with a thumb-nudge in the ribs. And the man-eater turned on me. You know the South Seas, and you know that the tiger shark, like the bald-face grizzly of Alaska, never gives trail. The combat, fathoms deep under the sea, was on—if by combat may be named such a one-sided struggle.

"The Princess unaware, caught her squid and rose to the surface. The man-eater rushed me. I fended him off with both hands on his nose above his thousand-toothed open mouth, so that he backed me against the sharp coral. The scars are there to this day. Whenever I tried to rise, he rushed me, and I could not remain down there indefinitely without air. Whenever he rushed me, I fended him off with my hands on his nose. And I would have escaped unharmed, except for the slip of my right hand. Into his mouth it went to the elbow. His jaws closed, just below the elbow. You know how a shark's teeth are. Once in they cannot be released. They must go through to complete the bite, but they cannot go through heavy bone. So, from just below the elbow he stripped the bone clean to the articulation of the wrist-joint, where his teeth met and my good right hand became his for an appetizer.

"But while he was doing this, I drove the thumb of my left hand, to the hilt into his eye-orifice and popped out his eye. This did not stop him. The meat had maddened him. He pursued the gushing stump of my wrist. Half a dozen times I fended with my intact arm. Then he got the poor mangled arm again, closed down, and stripped the meat off the bone from the shoulder down to the elbow-joint, where his teeth met and he was free of his second mouthful of me. But, at the same time, with my good arm, I thumbed out his remaining eye."

Percival Delaney shrugged his shoulders, ere he resumed.

"From above, those in the canoe had beheld the entire happening and were loud in praise of my deed. To this day they still sing the song of me, and tell the tale of me. And the Princess." His pause was brief but significant. "The Princess married me. . . . Oh, well-a-day and lack-a-day, the whirligig of time and fortune, the topsyturviness of luck, the wooden shoe going up and the polished heel descending a French gunboat, a conquered island kingdom of Oceania, to-day ruled over by a peasant-born, unlettered, colonial gendarme, and . . ."

He completed the sentence and the tale by burying his face in the down-tilted mouth of the condensed milk can and by gurgling the corrosive drink down his throat in thirsty gulps.

After an appropriate pause, Chauncey Delarouse, otherwise Whiskers, took up the tale.

"Far be it from me to boast of no matter what place of birth I have descended from to sit here by this fire with such as . . . as chance along. I may say, however, that I, too, was once a considerable figure of a man. I may add that it was horses, plus parents too indulgent, that exiled me out over the world. I may still wonder to query: 'Are Dover's cliffs still white?'"

"Huh!" Bruce Cadogan Cavendish sneered. "Next you'll be asking: 'How fares the old Lord Warden?'"

"And I took every liberty, and vainly, with a constitution that was iron," Whiskers hurried on. "Here I am with my three score and ten behind me, and back on that long road have I buried many a youngster that was as rare and devilish as I, but who could not stand the pace. I knew the worst too young. And now I know the worst too old. But there was a time, alas all too short, when I knew, the best.

"I, too, kiss my hand to the Princess of my heart. She was truly a princess, Polynesian, a thousand miles and more away to the eastward and the south from Delaney's Isle of Love. The natives of all around that part of the South Seas called it the Jolly Island. Their own name, the name of the people who dwelt thereon, translates delicately and justly into 'The Island of Tranquil Laughter.' On the chart you will find the erroneous name given to it by the old navigators to be Manatomana. The seafaring gentry the round ocean around called it the Adamless Eden. And the missionaries for a time called it God's Witness—so great had been their success at converting the inhabitants. As for me, it was, and ever shall be, Paradise.

"It was MY Paradise, for it was there my Princess lived. John Asibeli Tungi was king. He was full-blooded native, descended out of the oldest and highest chief-stock that traced back to Manua which was the primeval sea home of the race. Also was he known as John the Apostate. He lived a long life and apostasized frequently. First converted by the Catholics, he threw down the idols, broke the tabus, cleaned out the native priests, executed a few of the recalcitrant ones, and sent all his subjects to church.

"Next he fell for the traders, who developed in him a champagne thirst, and he shipped off the Catholic priests to New Zealand. The great majority of his subjects always followed his lead, and, having no religion at all, ensued the time of the Great Licentiousness, when by all South Seas missionaries his island, in sermons, was spoken of as Babylon.

"But the traders ruined his digestion with too much champagne, and after several years he fell for the Gospel according to the Methodists, sent his people to church, and cleaned up the beach and the trading crowd so spick and span that he would not permit them to smoke a pipe out of doors on Sunday, and, fined one of the chief traders one hundred gold sovereigns for washing his schooner's decks on the Sabbath morn.

"That was the time of the Blue Laws, but perhaps it was too rigorous for King John. Off he packed the Methodists, one fine day, exiled several hundred of his people to Samoa for sticking to Methodism, and, of all things, invented a religion of his own, with himself the figure-head of worship. In this he was aided and abetted by a renegade Fijian. This lasted five years. Maybe he grew tired of being God, or maybe it was because the Fijian decamped with the six thousand pounds in the royal treasury; but at any rate the Second Reformed Wesleyans got him, and his entire kingdom went Wesleyan. The pioneer Wesleyan missionary he actually made prime minister, and what he did to the trading crowd was a caution. Why, in the end, King John's kingdom was blacklisted and boycotted by the traders till the revenues diminished to zero, the people went bankrupt, and King John couldn't borrow a shilling from his most powerful chief.

"By this time he was getting old, and philosophic, and tolerant, and spiritually atavistic. He fired out the Second Reformed Wesleyans, called back the exiles from Samoa, invited in the traders, held a general love-feast, took the lid off, proclaimed religious liberty and high tariff, and as for himself went back to the worship of his ancestors, dug up the idols, reinstated a few octogenarian priests, and observed the tabus. All of which was lovely for the traders, and prosperity reigned. Of course, most of his subjects followed him back into heathen worship. Yet quite a sprinkling of Catholics, Methodists and Wesleyans remained true to their beliefs and managed to maintain a few squalid, one-horse churches. But King John didn't mind, any more than did he the high times of the traders along the beach. Everything went, so long as the taxes were paid. Even when his wife, Queen Mamare, elected to become a Baptist, and invited in a little, weazened, sweet-spirited, club-footed Baptist missionary, King John did not object. All he insisted on was that these wandering religions should be self-supporting and not feed a pennyworth's out of the royal coffers.

"And now the threads of my recital draw together in the paragon of female exquisiteness—my Princess."

Whiskers paused, placed carefully on the ground his half-full condensed milk can with which he had been absently toying, and kissed the fingers of his one hand audibly aloft.

"She was the daughter of Queen Mamare. She was the woman wonderful. Unlike the Diana type of Polynesian, she was almost ethereal. She WAS ethereal, sublimated by purity, as shy and modest as a violet, as fragile-slender as a lily, and her eyes, luminous and shrinking tender, were as asphodels on the sward of heaven. She was all flower, and fire, and dew. Hers was the sweetness of the mountain rose, the gentleness of the dove. And she was all of good as well as all of beauty, devout in her belief in her mother's worship, which was the worship introduced by Ebenezer Naismith, the Baptist missionary. But make no mistake. She was no mere sweet spirit ripe for the bosom of Abraham. All of exquisite deliciousness of woman was she. She was woman, all woman, to the last sensitive quivering atom of her -

"And I? I was a wastrel of the beach. The wildest was not so wild as I, the keenest not so keen, of all that wild, keen trading crowd. It was esteemed I played the stiffest hand of poker. I was the only living man, white, brown, or black, who dared run the Kuni-kuni Passage in the dark. And on a black night I have done it under reefs in a gale of wind. Well, anyway, I had a bad reputation on a beach where there were no good reputations. I was reckless, dangerous, stopped at nothing in fight or frolic; and the trading captains used to bring boiler-sheeted prodigies from the vilest holes of the South Pacific to try and drink me under the table. I remember one, a calcined Scotchman from the New Hebrides. It was a great drinking. He died of it, and we laded him aboard ship, pickled in a cask of trade rum, and sent him back to his own place. A sample, a fair sample, of the antic tricks we cut up on the beach of Manatomana.

"And of all unthinkable things, what did I up and do, one day, but look upon the Princess to find her good and to fall in love with her. It was the real thing. I was as mad as a March hare, and after that I got only madder. I reformed. Think of that! Think of what a slip of a woman can do to a busy, roving man!—By the Lord Harry, it's true. I reformed. I went to church. Hear me! I became converted. I cleared my soul before God and kept my hands—I had two then—off the ribald crew of the beach when it laughed at this, my latest antic, and wanted to know what was my game.

"I tell ou I reformed, and gave myself in passion and sincerity to a religious experience that has made me tolerant of all religion ever since. I discharged my best captain for immorality. So did I my cook, and a better never boiled water in Manatomana. For the same reason I discharged my chief clerk. And for the first time in the history of trading my schooners to the westward carried Bibles in their stock. I built a little anchorite bungalow up town on a mango-lined street squarely alongside the little house occupied by Ebenezer Naismith. And I made him my pal and comrade, and found him a veritable honey pot of sweetnesses and goodnesses. And he was a man, through and through a man. And he died long after like a man, which I would like to tell you about, were the tale of it not so deservedly long.

"It was the Princess, more than the missionary, who was responsible for my expressing my faith in works, and especially in that crowning work, the New Church, Our Church, the Queen-mother's church.

"'Our poor church,' she said to me, one night after prayer-meeting. I had been converted only a fortnight. 'It is so small its congregation can never grow. And the roof leaks. And King John, my hard-hearted father, will not contribute a penny. Yet he has a big balance in the treasury. And Manatomana is not poor. Much money is made and squandered, I know. I hear the gossip of the wild ways of the beach. Less than a month ago you lost more in one night, gambling at cards, than the cost of the upkeep of our poor church for a year.'"

"And I told her it was true, but that it was before I had seen the light. (I'd had an infernal run of bad luck.) I told her I had not tasted liquor since, nor turned a card. I told her that the roof would be repaired at once, by Christian carpenters selected by her from the congregation. But she was filled with the thought of a great revival that Ebenezer Naismith could preach—she was a dear saint—and she spoke of a great church, saying:

"'You are rich. You have many schooners, and traders in far

islands, and I have heard of a great contract you have signed to recruit labour for the German plantations of Upolu. They say, next to Sweitzer, you are the richest trader here. I should love to see some use of all this money placed to the glory of God. It would be a noble thing to do, and I should be proud to know the man who would do it.'"

"I told her that Ebenezer Naismith would preach the revival, and that I would build a church great enough in which to house it.

"As big as the Catholic church?" she asked.

"This was the ruined cathedral, built at the time when the entire population was converted, and it was a large order; but I was afire with love, and I told her that the church I would build would be even bigger.

"'But it will take money,' I explained. 'And it takes time to make money.'"

"'You have much,' she said. 'Some say you have more money than my father, the King.'"

"'I have more credit,' I explained. 'But you do not understand money. It takes money to have credit. So, with the money I have, and the credit I have, I will work to make more money and credit, and the church shall be built.'"

"Work! I was a surprise to myself. It is an amazement, the amount of time a man finds on his hands after he's given up carousing, and gambling, and all the time-eating diversions of the beach. And I didn't waste a second of all my new-found time. Instead I worked it overtime. I did the work of half a dozen men. I became a driver. My captains made faster runs than ever and earned bigger bonuses, as did my supercargoes, who saw to it that my schooners did not loaf and dawdle along the way. And I saw to it that my supercargoes did see to it.

"And good! By the Lord Harry I was so good it hurt. My conscience got so expansive and fine-strung it lamed me across the shoulders to carry it around with me. Why, I even went back over my accounts and paid Sweitzer fifty quid I'd jiggered him out of in a deal in Fiji three years before. And I compounded the interest as well.

"Work! I planted sugar cane—the first commercial planting on Manatomana. I ran in cargoes of kinky-heads from Malaita, which is in the Solomons, till I had twelve hundred of the blackbirds putting in cane. And I sent a schooner clear to Hawaii to bring back a dismantled sugar mill and a German who said he knew the field-end of cane. And he did, and he charged me three hundred dollars screw a month, and I took hold of the mill-end. I installed the mill myself, with the help of several mechanics I brought up from Queensland.

"Of course there was a rival. His name was Motomoe. He was the very highest chief blood next to King John's. He was full native, a strapping, handsome man, with a glowering way of showing his dislikes. He certainly glowered at me when I began hanging around the palace. He went back in my history and circulated the blackest tales about me. The worst of it was that most of them were true. He even made a voyage to Apia to find things out—as if he couldn't find a plenty right there on the beach of Manatomana! And he sneered at my failing for religion, and at my going to prayer-meeting, and, most of all, at my sugar-planting. He challenged me to fight, and I kept off of him. He threatened me, and I learned in the nick of time of his plan to have me knocked on the head. You see, he wanted the Princess just as much as I did, and I wanted her more.

"She used to play the piano. So did I, once. But I never let her know after I'd heard her play the first time. And she thought her playing was wonderful, the dear, fond girl! You know the sort, the mechanical one-two-three tum-tum-tum school-girl stuff. And now I'll tell you something funnier. Her playing WAS wonderful to me. The gates of heaven opened to me when she played. I can see myself now, worn out and dog-tired after the long day, lying on the mats of the palace veranda and gazing upon her at the piano, myself in a perfect idiocy of bliss. Why, this idea she had of her fine playing was the one flaw in her deliciousness of perfection, and I loved her for it. It kind of brought her within my human reach. Why, when she played her one-two-three, tum-tum-tum, I was in the seventh heaven of bliss. My weariness fell from me. I loved her, and my love for her was clean as flame, clean as my love for God. And do you know, into my fond lover's fancy continually intruded the thought that God in most ways must look like her.

"—That's right, Bruce Cadogan Cavendish, sneer as you like. But I tell you that's love that I've been describing. That's all. It's love. It's the realest, purest, finest thing that can happen to a man. And I know what I'm talking about. It happened to me."

Whiskers, his beady squirrel's eye glittering from out his ruined eyebrow like a live coal in a jungle ambush, broke off long enough to down a sedative draught from his condensed milk can and to mix another.

"The cane," he resumed, wiping his prodigious mat of face hair with the back of his hand. "It matured in sixteen months in that climate, and I was ready, just ready and no more, with the mill for the grinding. Naturally, it did not all mature at once, but I had planted in such succession that I could grind for nine months steadily, while more was being planted and the ratoons were springing up.

"I had my troubles the first several days. If it wasn't one thing the matter with the mill, it was another. On the fourth day, Ferguson, my engineer, had to shut down several hours in order to remedy his own troubles. I was bothered by the feeder. After having the niggers (who had been feeding the cane) pour cream of lime on the rollers to keep everything sweet, I sent them out to join the cane-cutting squads. So I was all alone at that end, just as Ferguson started up the mill, just as I discovered what was the matter with the feed-rollers, and just as Motomoe strolled up.

"He stood there, in Norfolk jacket, pigskin puttees, and all the rest of the fashionable get-up out of a bandbox, sneering at me covered with filth and grease to the eyebrows and looking like a navvy. And, the rollers now white from the lime, I'd just seen what was wrong. The rollers were not in plumb. One side crushed the cane well, but the other side was too open. I shoved my fingers in on that side. The big, toothed cogs on the rollers did not touch my fingers. And yet, suddenly, they did. With the grip of ten thousand devils, my finger-tips were caught, drawn in, and pulped to—well, just pulp. And, like a slick of cane, I had started on my way. There was no stopping me. Ten thousand horses could not have pulled me back. There was nothing to stop me. Hand, arm, shoulder, head, and chest, down to the toes of me, I was doomed to feed through.

"It did hurt. It hurt so much it did not hurt me at all. Quite detached, almost may I say, I looked on my hand being ground up, knuckle by knuckle, joint by joint, the back of the hand, the wrist, the forearm, all in order slowly and inevitably feeding in. O engineer hoist by thine own petard! O sugar-maker crushed by thine own cane-crusher!

"Motomoe sprang forward involuntarily, and the sneer was chased from his face by an expression of solicitude. Then the beauty of the situation dawned on him, and he chuckled and grinned. No, I didn't expect anything of him. Hadn't he tried to knock me on the head? What could he do anyway? He didn't know anything about engines.

"I yelled at the top of my lungs to Ferguson to shut off the engine, but the roar of the machinery drowned my voice. And there I stood, up to the elbow and feeding right on in. Yes, it did hurt. There were some astonishing twinges when special nerves were shredded and dragged out by the roots. But I remember that I was surprised at the time that it did not hurt worse.

"Motomoe made a movement that attracted my attention. At the same time he growled out loud, as if he hated himself, 'I'm a fool.' What he had done was to pick up a cane-knife—you know the kind, as big as a machete and as heavy. And I was grateful to him in advance for putting me out of my misery. There wasn't any sense in slowly feeding in till my head was crushed, and already my arm was pulped half way from elbow to shoulder, and the pulping was going right on. So I was grateful, as I bent my head to the blow.

"Get your head out of the way, you idiot!" he barked at me.

"And then I understood and obeyed. I was a big man, and he took two hacks to do it; but he hacked my arm off just outside the shoulder and dragged me back and laid me down on the cane.

"Yes, the sugar paid—enormously; and I built for the Princess the church of her saintly dream, and . . . she married me."

He partly assuaged his thirst, and uttered his final word.

"Alackaday! Shuttlecock and battle-dore. And this at, the end of it all, lined with boilerplate that even alcohol will not corrode and that only alcohol will tickle. Yet have I lived, and I kiss my hand to the dear dust of my Princess long asleep in the great mausoleum of King John that looks across the Vale of Manona to the alien flag that floats over the bungalow of the British Government House. . . "

Fatty pledged him sympathetically, and sympathetically drank out of his own small can. Bruce Cadogan Cavendish glared into the fire with implacable bitterness. He was a man who preferred to drink by himself. Across the thin lips that composed the cruel slash of his mouth played twitches of mockery that caught Fatty's eye. And Fatty, making sure first that his rock-chunk was within reach, challenged.

"Well, how about yourself, Bruce Cadogan Cavendish? It's

your turn."

The other lifted bleak eyes that bored into Fatty's until he physically betrayed uncomfortableness.

"I've lived a hard life," Slim grated harshly. "What do I know about love passages?"

"No man of your build and make-up could have escaped them," Fatty wheedled.

"And what of it?" Slim snarled. "It's no reason for a gentleman to boast of amorous triumphs."

"Oh, go on, be a good fellow," Fatty urged. "The night's still young. We've still some drink left. Delarouse and I have contributed our share. It isn't often that three real ones like us get together for a telling. Surely you've got at least one adventure in love you aren't ashamed to tell about—"

Bruce Cadogan Cavendish pulled forth his iron quoit and seemed to debate whether or not he should brain the other. He sighed, and put back the quoit.

"Very well, if you will have it," he surrendered with manifest reluctance. "Like you two, I have had a remarkable constitution. And right now, speaking of armour-plate lining, I could drink the both of you down when you were at your prime. Like you two, my beginnings were far distant and different. That I am marked with the hall-mark of gentlehood there is no discussion . . . unless either of you care to discuss the matter now . . . "

His one hand slipped into his pocket and clutched the quoit. Neither of his auditors spoke nor betrayed any awareness of his menace.

"It occurred a thousand miles to the westward of Manatomana, on the island of Tagalag," he continued abruptly, with an air of saturnine disappointment in that there had been no discussion. "But first I must tell you of how I got to Tagalag. For reasons I shall not mention, by paths of descent I shall not describe, in the crown of my manhood and the prime of my devilishness in which Oxford renegades and racing younger sons had nothing on me, I found myself master and owner of a schooner so well known that she shall remain historically nameless. I was running blackbird labour from the west South Pacific and the Coral Sea to the plantations of Hawaii and the nitrate mines of Chili—"

"It was you who cleaned out the entire population of—" Fatty exploded, ere he could check his speech.

The one hand of Bruce Cadogan Cavendish flashed pocket-ward and flashed back with the quoit balanced ripe for business.

"Proceed," Fatty sighed. "I . . . I have quite forgotten what I was going to say."

"Beastly funny country over that way," the narrator drawled with perfect casualness. "You've read this Sea Wolf stuff—"

"You weren't the Sea Wolf," Whiskers broke in with involuntary positiveness.

"No, sir," was the snarling answer. "The Sea Wolf's dead, isn't he? And I'm still alive, aren't I?"

"Of course, of course," Whiskers conceded. "He suffocated head-first in the mud off a wharf in Victoria a couple of years back."

"As I was saying—and I don't like interruptions," Bruce Cadogan Cavendish proceeded, "it's a beastly funny country over that way. I was at Taki-Tiki, a low island that politically belongs to the Solomons, but that geologically doesn't at all, for the Solomons are high islands. Ethnographically it belongs to Polynesia, Melanesia, and Micronesia, because all the breeds of the South Pacific have gravitated to it by canoe-drift and intricately, degeneratively, and amazingly interbred. The scum of the scrapings of the bottom of the human pit, biologically speaking, resides in Taka-Tiki. And I know the bottom and whereof I speak.

"It was a beastly funny time of it I had, diving out shell, fishing beche-de-mer, trading hoop-iron and hatchets for copra and ivory-nuts, running niggers and all the rest of it. Why, even in Fiji the Lotu was having a hard time of it and the chiefs still eating long-pig. To the westward it was fierce— funny little black kinky- heads, man-eaters the last Jack of them, and the jackpot fat and spilling over with wealth—"

"Jack-pots?" Fatty queried. At sight of an irritable movement, he added: "You see, I never got over to the West like Delarouse and you."

"They're all head-hunters. Heads are valuable, especially a white man's head. They decorate the canoe-houses and devil-devil houses with them. Each village runs a jack-pot, and everybody antes. Whoever brings in a white man's head takes the pot. If there aren't openers for a long time, the pot grows to tremendous proportions. Beastly funny, isn't it?

"I know. Didn't a Holland mate die on me of blackwater? And didn't I win a pot myself? It was this way. We were lying at Lango-lui at the time. I never let on, and arranged the affair with Johnny, my boat-steerer. He was a kinky-head himself from Port Moresby. He cut the dead mate's head off and sneaked ashore in the might, while I whanged away with my rifle as if I were trying to get him. He opened the pot with the mate's head, and got it, too. Of course, next day I sent in a landing boat, with two covering boats, and fetched him off with the loot."

"How big was the pot?" Whiskers asked. "I heard of a pot at Orla worth eighty quid."

"To commence with," Slim answered, "there were forty fat pigs, each worth a fathom of prime shell-money, and shell-money worth a quid a fathom. That was two hundred dollars right there. There were ninety-eight fathoms of shell-money, which is pretty close to five hundred in itself. And there were twenty-two gold sovereigns. I split it four ways: one-fourth to Johnny, one-fourth to the ship, one-fourth to me as owner, and one-fourth to me as skipper. Johnny never complained. He'd never had so much wealth all at one time in his life. Besides, I gave him a couple of the mate's old shirts. And I fancy the mate's head is still there decorating the canoe-house."

"Not exactly Christian burial of a Christian," Whiskers observed.

"But a lucrative burial," Slim retorted. "I had to feed the rest of the mate over-side to the sharks for nothing. Think of feeding an eight-hundred-dollar head along with it. It would have been criminal waste and stark lunacy.

"Well, anyway, it was all beastly funny, over there to the westward. And, without telling you the scrape I got into at Taki-Tiki, except that I sailed away with two hundred kinky-heads for Queensland labour, and for my manner of collecting them had two British ships of war combing the Pacific for me, I changed my course and ran to the westward thinking to dispose of the lot to the Spanish plantations on Bangar.

"Typhoon season. We caught it. The Merry Mist was my schooner's name, and I had thought she was stoutly built until she hit that typhoon. I never saw such seas. They pounded that stout craft to pieces, literally so. The sticks were jerked out of her, deckhouses splintered to match-wood, rails ripped off, and, after the worst had passed, the covering boards began to go. We just managed to repair what was left of one boat and keep the schooner afloat only till the sea went down barely enough to get away. And we outfitted that boat in a hurry. The carpenter and I were the last, and we had to jump for it as he went down. There were only four of us—"

"Lost all the niggers?" Whiskers inquired.

"Some of them swam for some time," Slim replied. "But I don't fancy they made the land. We were ten days' in doing it. And we had a spanking breeze most of the way. And what do you think we had in the boat with us? Cases of square-face gin and cases of dynamite. Funny, wasn't it? Well, it got funnier later on. Oh, there was a small beaker of water, a little salt horse, and some salt-water-soaked sea biscuit—enough to keep us alive to Tagalag.

"Now Tagalag is the disappointingest island I've ever beheld. It shows up out of the sea so as you can make its fall twenty miles off. It is a volcano cone thrust up out of deep sea, with a segment of the crater wall broken out. This gives sea entrance to the crater itself, and makes a fine sheltered harbour. And that's all. Nothing lives there. The outside and the inside of the crater are too steep. At one place, inside, is a patch of about a thousand coconut palms. And that's all, as I said, saving a few insects. No four-legged thing, even a rat, inhabits the place. And it's funny, most awful funny, with all those coconuts, not even a coconut crab. The only meat-food living was schools of mullet in the harbour—fattest, finest, biggest mullet I ever laid eyes on.

"And the four of us landed on the little beach and set up housekeeping among the coconuts with a larder full of dynamite and square-face. Why don't you laugh? It's funny, I tell you. Try it some time.—Holland gin and straight coconut diet. I've never been able to look a confectioner's window in the face since. Now I'm not strong on religion like Chauncey Delarouse there, but I have some primitive ideas; and my concept of hell is an illimitable coconut plantation, stocked with cases of square-face and populated by ship-wrecked mariners. Funny? It must make the devil scream.

"You know, straight coconut is what the agriculturists call an unbalanced ration. It certainly unbalanced our digestions. We got so that whenever hunger took an extra bite at us, we took another drink of gin. After a couple of weeks of it, Olaf, a squarehead sailor, got an idea. It came when he was full of gin, and we, being in the same fix, just watched him shove a cap and short fuse into a stick of dynamite and stroll down toward the boat.

"It dawned on me that he was going to shoot fish if there were any about; but the sun was beastly hot, and I just reclined there and hoped he'd have luck.

"About half an hour after he disappeared we heard the explosion. But he didn't come back. We waited till the cool of sunset, and down on the beach found what had become of him. The boat was there all right, grounded by the prevailing breeze, but there was no Olaf. He would never have to eat coconut again. We went back, shakier than ever, and cracked another square-face.

"The next day the cook announced that he would rather take his chance with dynamite than continue trying to exist on coconut, and that, though he didn't know anything about dynamite, he knew a sight too much about coconut. So we bit the detonator down for him, shoved in a fuse, and picked him a good fire-stick, while he jolted up with a couple more stiff ones of gin.

"It was the same programme as the day before. After a while we heard the explosion and at twilight went down to the boat, from which we scraped enough of the cook for a funeral.

"The carpenter and I stuck it out two days more, then we drew straws for it and it was his turn. We parted with harsh words; for he wanted to take a square-face along to refresh himself by the way, while I was set against running any chance of wasting the gin. Besides, he had more than he could carry then, and he wobbled and staggered as he walked.

"Same thing, only there was a whole lot of him left for me to bury, because he'd prepared only half a stick. I managed to last it out till next day, when, after duly fortifying myself, I got sufficient courage to tackle the dynamite. I used only a third of a stick—you know, short fuse, with the end split so as to hold the head of a safety match. That's where I mended my predecessors' methods. Not using the match-head, they'd too-long fuses. Therefore, when they spotted a school of mullet; and lighted the fuse, they had to hold the dynamite till the fuse burned short before they threw it. If they threw it too soon, it wouldn't go off the instant it hit the water, while the splash of it would frighten the mullet away. Funny stuff dynamite. At any rate, I still maintain mine was the safer method.

"I picked up a school of mullet before I'd been rowing five minutes. Fine big fat ones they were, and I could smell them over the fire. When I stood up, fire-stick in one hand, dynamite stick in the other, my knees were knocking together. Maybe it was the gin, or the anxiousness, or the weakness and the hunger, and maybe it was the result of all of them, but at any rate I was all of a shake. Twice I failed to touch the fire-stick to the dynamite. Then I did, heard the match-head splutter, and let her go.

"Now I don't know what happened to the others, but I know what I did. I got turned about. Did you ever stem a strawberry and throw the strawberry away and pop the stem into your mouth? That's what I did. I threw the fire-stick into the water after the mullet and held on to the dynamite. And my arm went off with the stick when it went off. . . . "

Slim investigated the tomato-can for water to mix himself a drink, but found it empty. He stood up.

"Heigh ho," he yawned, and started down the path to the river.

In several minutes he was back. He mixed the due quantity of river slush with the alcohol, took a long, solitary drink, and stared with bitter moodiness into the fire.

"Yes, but . . . " Fatty suggested. "What happened then?"

"Oh," sad Slim. "Then the princess married me, of course."

"But you were the only person left, and there wasn't any princess . . . " Whiskers cried out abruptly, and then let his voice trail away to embarrassed silence.

Slim stared unblinkingly into the fire.

Percival Delaney and Chauncey Delarouse looked at each other. Quietly, in solemn silence, each with his one arm aided the one arm of the other in rolling and tying his bundle. And in silence, bundles slung on shoulders, they went away out of the circle of firelight. Not until they reached the top of the railroad embankment did they speak.

"No gentleman would have done it," said Whiskers.

"No gentleman would have done it," Fatty agreed.

Glen Ellen, California, September 26, 1916.

ABOUT THE AUTHOR

 **Jack London,** probably born John Griffith Chaney (January 12, 1876 – November 22, 1916) was an American author who wrote The Call of the Wild and over fifty other books. A pioneer in the then-burgeoning world of commercial magazine fiction, he was one of the first Americans to make a huge financial success from writing.

Clarice Stasz and other biographers believe it to be likely that Jack London's biological father was astrologer William Chaney. Chaney was a professor of astrology; according to Stasz, "From the viewpoint of serious astrologers today, Chaney is a major figure who shifted the practice from quackery to a more rigorous method."

A pivotal event was his discovery in 1886 of the Oakland Public Library and a sympathetic librarian, Ina Coolbrith (who later became California's first poet laureate and an important figure in the San Francisco literary community).

In later life Jack London indulged his very wide-ranging interests with a personal library of 15,000 volumes, referring to his books as "the tools of my trade."

Choose from Thousands of 1stWorldLibrary Classics By

A. M. Barnard
Ada Leverson
Adolphus William Ward
Aesop
Agatha Christie
Alexander Aaronsohn
Alexander Kielland
Alexandre Dumas
Alfred Gatty
Alfred Ollivant
Alice Duer Miller
Alice Turner Curtis
Alice Dunbar
Allen Chapman
Alleyne Ireland
Ambrose Bierce
Amelia E. Barr
Amory H. Bradford
Andrew Lang
Andrew McFarland Davis
Andy Adams
Angela Brazil
Anna Alice Chapin
Anna Sewell
Annie Besant
Annie Hamilton Donnell
Annie Payson Call
Annie Roe Carr
Annonaymous
Anton Chekhov
Archibald Lee Fletcher
Arnold Bennett
Arthur C. Benson
Arthur Conan Doyle
Arthur M. Winfield
Arthur Ransome
Arthur Schnitzler
Arthur Train
Atticus
B.H. Baden-Powell
B. M. Bower
B. C. Chatterjee
Baroness Emmuska Orczy
Baroness Orczy
Basil King
Bayard Taylor
Ben Macomber
Bertha Muzzy Bower
Bjornstjerne Bjornson

Booth Tarkington
Boyd Cable
Bram Stoker
C. Collodi
C. E. Orr
C. M. Ingleby
Carolyn Wells
Catherine Parr Traill
Charles A. Eastman
Charles Amory Beach
Charles Dickens
Charles Dudley Warner
Charles Farrar Browne
Charles Ives
Charles Kingsley
Charles Klein
Charles Hanson Towne
Charles Lathrop Pack
Charles Romyn Dake
Charles Whibley
Charles Willing Beale
Charlotte M. Braeme
Charlotte M. Yonge
Charlotte Perkins Stetson
Clair W. Hayes
Clarence Day Jr.
Clarence E. Mulford
Clemence Housman
Confucius
Coningsby Dawson
Cornelis DeWitt Wilcox
Cyril Burleigh
D. H. Lawrence
Daniel Defoe
David Garnett
Dinah Craik
Don Carlos Janes
Donald Keyhoe
Dorothy Kilner
Dougan Clark
Douglas Fairbanks
E. Nesbit
E. P. Roe
E. Phillips Oppenheim
E. S. Brooks
Earl Barnes
Edgar Rice Burroughs
Edith Van Dyne
Edith Wharton

Edward Everett Hale
Edward J. O'Biren
Edward S. Ellis
Edwin L. Arnold
Eleanor Atkins
Eleanor Hallowell Abbott
Eliot Gregory
Elizabeth Gaskell
Elizabeth McCracken
Elizabeth Von Arnim
Ellem Key
Emerson Hough
Emilie F. Carlen
Emily Bronte
Emily Dickinson
Enid Bagnold
Enilor Macartney Lane
Erasmus W. Jones
Ernie Howard Pie
Ethel May Dell
Ethel Turner
Ethel Watts Mumford
Eugene Sue
Eugenie Foa
Eugene Wood
Eustace Hale Ball
Evelyn Everett-green
Everard Cotes
F. H. Cheley
F. J. Cross
F. Marion Crawford
Fannie E. Newberry
Federick Austin Ogg
Ferdinand Ossendowski
Fergus Hume
Florence A. Kilpatrick
Fremont B. Deering
Francis Bacon
Francis Darwin
Frances Hodgson Burnett
Frances Parkinson Keyes
Frank Gee Patchin
Frank Harris
Frank Jewett Mather
Frank L. Packard
Frank V. Webster
Frederic Stewart Isham
Frederick Trevor Hill
Frederick Winslow Taylor

Friedrich Kerst	Hayden Carruth	James Branch Cabell
Friedrich Nietzsche	Helent Hunt Jackson	James DeMille
Fyodor Dostoyevsky	Helen Nicolay	James Joyce
G.A. Henty	Hendrik Conscience	James Lane Allen
G.K. Chesterton	Hendy David Thoreau	James Lane Allen
Gabrielle E. Jackson	Henri Barbusse	James Oliver Curwood
Garrett P. Serviss	Henrik Ibsen	James Oppenheim
Gaston Leroux	Henry Adams	James Otis
George A. Warren	Henry Ford	James R. Driscoll
George Ade	Henry Frost	Jane Abbott
Geroge Bernard Shaw	Henry James	Jane Austen
George Cary Eggleston	Henry Jones Ford	Jane L. Stewart
George Durston	Henry Seton Merriman	Janet Aldridge
George Ebers	Henry W Longfellow	Jens Peter Jacobsen
George Eliot	Herbert A. Giles	Jerome K. Jerome
George Gissing	Herbert Carter	Jessie Graham Flower
George MacDonald	Herbert N. Casson	John Buchan
George Meredith	Herman Hesse	John Burroughs
George Orwell	Hildegard G. Frey	John Cournos
George Sylvester Viereck	Homer	John F. Kennedy
George Tucker	Honore De Balzac	John Gay
George W. Cable	Horace B. Day	John Glasworthy
George Wharton James	Horace Walpole	John Habberton
Gertrude Atherton	Horatio Alger Jr.	John Joy Bell
Gordon Casserly	Howard Pyle	John Kendrick Bangs
Grace E. King	Howard R. Garis	John Milton
Grace Gallatin	Hugh Lofting	John Philip Sousa
Grace Greenwood	Hugh Walpole	John Taintor Foote
Grant Allen	Humphry Ward	Jonas Lauritz Idemil Lie
Guillermo A. Sherwell	Ian Maclaren	Jonathan Swift
Gulielma Zollinger	Inez Haynes Gillmore	Joseph A. Altsheler
Gustav Flaubert	Irving Bacheller	Joseph Carey
H. A. Cody	Isabel Cecilia Williams	Joseph Conrad
H. B. Irving	Isabel Hornibrook	Joseph E. Badger Jr
H.C. Bailey	Israel Abrahams	Joseph Hergesheimer
H. G. Wells	Ivan Turgenev	Joseph Jacobs
H. H. Munro	J.G.Austin	Jules Vernes
H. Irving Hancock	J. Henri Fabre	Julian Hawthrone
H. R. Naylor	J. M. Barrie	Julie A Lippmann
H. Rider Haggard	J. M. Walsh	Justin Huntly McCarthy
H. W. C. Davis	J. Macdonald Oxley	Kakuzo Okakura
Haldeman Julius	J. R. Miller	Karle Wilson Baker
Hall Caine	J. S. Fletcher	Kate Chopin
Hamilton Wright Mabie	J. S. Knowles	Kenneth Grahame
Hans Christian Andersen	J. Storer Clouston	Kenneth McGaffey
Harold Avery	J. W. Duffield	Kate Langley Bosher
Harold McGrath	Jack London	Kate Langley Bosher
Harriet Beecher Stowe	Jacob Abbott	Katherine Cecil Thurston
Harry Castlemon	James Allen	Katherine Stokes
Harry Coghill	James Andrews	L. A. Abbot
Harry Houidini	James Baldwin	L. T. Meade

L. Frank Baum
Latta Griswold
Laura Dent Crane
Laura Lee Hope
Laurence Housman
Lawrence Beasley
Leo Tolstoy
Leonid Andreyev
Lewis Carroll
Lewis Sperry Chafer
Lilian Bell
Lloyd Osbourne
Louis Hughes
Louis Joseph Vance
Louis Tracy
Louisa May Alcott
Lucy Fitch Perkins
Lucy Maud Montgomery
Luther Benson
Lydia Miller Middleton
Lyndon Orr
M. Corvus
M. H. Adams
Margaret E. Sangster
Margret Howth
Margaret Vandercook
Margaret W. Hungerford
Margret Penrose
Maria Edgeworth
Maria Thompson Daviess
Mariano Azuela
Marion Polk Angellotti
Mark Overton
Mark Twain
Mary Austin
Mary Catherine Crowley
Mary Cole
Mary Hastings Bradley
Mary Roberts Rinehart
Mary Rowlandson
M. Wollstonecraft Shelley
Maud Lindsay
Max Beerbohm
Myra Kelly
Nathaniel Hawthrone
Nicolo Machiavelli
O. F. Walton
Oscar Wilde

Owen Johnson
P.G. Wodehouse
Paul and Mabel Thorne
Paul G. Tomlinson
Paul Severing
Percy Brebner
Percy Keese Fitzhugh
Peter B. Kyne
Plato
Quincy Allen
R. Derby Holmes
R. L. Stevenson
R. S. Ball
Rabindranath Tagore
Rahul Alvares
Ralph Bonehill
Ralph Henry Barbour
Ralph Victor
Ralph Waldo Emmerson
Rene Descartes
Ray Cummings
Rex Beach
Rex E. Beach
Richard Harding Davis
Richard Jefferies
Richard Le Gallienne
Robert Barr
Robert Frost
Robert Gordon Anderson
Robert L. Drake
Robert Lansing
Robert Lynd
Robert Michael Ballantyne
Robert W. Chambers
Rosa Nouchette Carey
Rudyard Kipling
Saint Augustine
Samuel B. Allison
Samuel Hopkins Adams
Sarah Bernhardt
Sarah C. Hallowell
Selma Lagerlof
Sherwood Anderson
Sigmund Freud
Standish O'Grady
Stanley Weyman
Stella Benson
Stella M. Francis

Stephen Crane
Stewart Edward White
Stijn Streuvels
Swami Abhedananda
Swami Parmananda
T. S. Ackland
T. S. Arthur
The Princess Der Ling
Thomas A. Janvier
Thomas A Kempis
Thomas Anderton
Thomas Bailey Aldrich
Thomas Bulfinch
Thomas De Quincey
Thomas Dixon
Thomas H. Huxley
Thomas Hardy
Thomas More
Thornton W. Burgess
U. S. Grant
Upton Sinclair
Valentine Williams
Various Authors
Vaughan Kester
Victor Appleton
Victor G. Durham
Victoria Cross
Virginia Woolf
Wadsworth Camp
Walter Camp
Walter Scott
Washington Irving
Wilbur Lawton
Wilkie Collins
Willa Cather
Willard F. Baker
William Dean Howells
William le Queux
W. Makepeace Thackeray
William W. Walter
William Shakespeare
Winston Churchill
Yei Theodora Ozaki
Yogi Ramacharaka
Young E. Allison
Zane Grey